TURBOTT WOLFE

WILLIAM PLOMER was born in Pietersburg in the Northern Transvaal in 1903. After his education in England at Rugby School, he temporarily became a trader in Zululand and an apprentice farmer on the border with Basutoland (now Lesotho). Later he settled in Japan, and at the age of twenty-five was offered the Chair of English Literature in the Imperial University. *Turbott Wolfe* was written when he was twenty-one, and was followed by a succession of novels, including *Sado* (1931) and *Ali the Lion* (1936), short stories, and poetry. In the 1960s he collaborated with Benjamin Britten on a number of librettos, including *Curlew River* (1964) and *The Prodigal Son* (1968). In 1968 he was awarded the CBE, and from 1968 to 1971 he was President of the Poetry Society. He died in 1973.

LAURENS VAN DER POST was born in South Africa in 1906. He completed his education there at the age of seventeen, and joined the Durban newspaper, the *Natal Advertiser*. At the same time he began his lifelong friendships with William Plomer and Roy Campbell, who were living at Sezela on the South Coast of Natal. Subsequently he has distinguished himself as a film producer, with such films as *The Story of C. G. Jung* (1971) and *All Africa Within Us* (1975), and as a writer, notably for *The Dark Eye of Africa* (1955), *The Lost World of the Kalahari* (1958), *The Seed and the Sower* (1962) and *Journey Into Russia* (1964). In 1947 he was awarded the CBE, and in 1981 he was knighted.

ALSO AVAILABLE IN

TWENTIETH-CENTURY CLASSICS

H. E. Bates   MY UNCLE SILAS
Adrian Bell   CORDUROY
Adrian Bell   SILVER LEY
Adrian Bell   THE CHERRY TREE
Hilaire Belloc   THE FOUR MEN
Arnold Bennett   RICEYMAN STEPS
Hermann Broch   THE DEATH OF VIRGIL
John Collier   HIS MONKEY WIFE
Ivy Compton-Burnett   A FATHER AND HIS FATE
Ivy Compton-Burnett   MANSERVANT AND MAIDSERVANT
Cyril Connolly   THE ROCK POOL
D. J. Enright   ACADEMIC YEAR
Walter de la Mare   MEMOIRS OF A MIDGET
Peter de Vries   THE MACKEREL PLAZA
Ford Madox Ford   THE FIFTH QUEEN
Robert Graves   SEVEN DAYS IN NEW CRETE
Patrick Hamilton   THE SLAVES OF SOLITUDE
A. P. Herbert   THE SECRET BATTLE
Patrick Leigh Fermor   THE VIOLINS OF SAINT-JACQUES
Sinclair Lewis   ELMER GANTRY
Rose Macaulay   THEY WERE DEFEATED
V. S. Pritchett   DEAD MEN LEADING
Rainer Maria Rilke   THE NOTEBOOKS OF
MALTE LAURIDS BRIGGE
Saki   THE UNBEARABLE BASSINGTON
Lytton Strachey   ELIZABETH AND ESSEX
Rex Warner   THE AERODROME
Denton Welch   IN YOUTH IS PLEASURE
H. G. Wells   KIPPS
H. G. Wells   LOVE AND MR LEWISHAM
Edith Wharton   ETHAN FROME *and* SUMMER
Leonard Woolf   THE VILLAGE IN THE JUNGLE

WILLIAM PLOMER

Turbott Wolfe

━◄◄◄◆►►►━

INTRODUCED BY
LAURENS VAN DER POST

Oxford   New York
OXFORD UNIVERSITY PRESS
1985

Oxford University Press, Walton Street, Oxford OX2 6DP

London New York Toronto
Delhi Bombay Calcutta Madras Karachi
Kuala Lumpur Singapore Hong Kong Tokyo
Nairobi Dar es Salaam Cape Town
Melbourne Auckland

and associated companies in
Beirut Berlin Ibadan Mexico City Nicosia

Oxford is a trade mark of Oxford University Press

First published 1925 by The Hogarth Press
First issued as an Oxford University Press paperback 1985

British Library Cataloguing in Publication Data

Plomer, William
Turbott Wolfe.—(Twentieth-century classics)
I. Title II. Series
823 [F] PR6031.L7
ISBN 0-19-281890-2

Library of Congress Cataloging in Publication Data

Plomer, William, 1903–1973.
Turbott Wolfe.
(Twentieth-century classics)
I. Title II. Series
PR9369.3.P65T8 1985 823'.912 84-27266
ISBN 0-19-281890-2 (pbk.)

Printed in Great Britain by
Richard Clay (the Chaucer Press) Ltd.
Bungay, Suffolk

CONTENTS

As for the native, he reads his overlord with a single penetrating glance; he sees in him the illusion of civilization and humanity and he knows that they are non-existent. While he gives him the title of lord and the homage due to the master, he is profoundly conscious of his democratic, commercial nature and despises him for it in silence and judges him with a smile which his brother understands; and he too smiles. Never does he offend against the form of slavish servility; and, with his salaam, he acts as though he were the inferior, but he is silently aware that he is the superior.

LOUIS COUPERUS
translated by A.T. de Mattos

When the unconscious of a whole continent and age has made of itself poetry in the nightmare of a single, prophetic dreamer, when it has issued in his awful, bloodcurdling scream, one can of course consider this scream from the standpoint of a singing-teacher.

HERMANN HESSE
translated by Stephen Hudson

THE "TURBOTT WOLFE" AFFAIR

LAURENS VAN DER POST

WILLIAM PLOMER himself needs no introduction here. He has been writing now for close on forty years and long since has established a reputation that is unique in the literature of our time. I myself know of no sensibility engaged to-day in this exacting traffic with the meaningful word which is writing, that is at once so naturally committed to it, so sustained, and so independent of fashion and faction as is his. The list of his published works alone conveys this; five novels and four volumes of short stories; two biographies and two autobiographical books; a *Collected Poems*, and the librettos for two of Benjamin Britten's operas; the editing of various books, among them three diaries, one, the famous Kilvert's Diary, running to three volumes, as well as the papers left behind by our friend, the rare and gifted Anthony Butts. His editing of diaries of men no longer living constitutes in itself a considerable act of re-creation. Indeed the way in which he has diverted an urgent imagination from its proper task in order to deliver the untimely dead from their silence and give them once again a voice in the minds of living men, is for me among the most moving of his achievements. On such a record an octogenarian might well look back with a feeling of fulfilment. In a man of barely sixty years whose writing was impeded by nearly six years of service at the Admiralty in the War, it is remarkable. But what does, I fear, need re-introduction is this book *Turbott Wolfe* on which his reputation was founded. It has long been out of print and has vanished from the shelves of libraries, except possibly a South African library—one where, as a by-product of the violent disapproval which kept it under lock and key, it is ironically preserved from wear and tear. Considering the impact this book made and the consequences that flowed from it, the only surprising thing is that it has not been republished before.

Turbott Wolfe, published when William Plomer was twenty-two, was his first novel as well as his first book. He finished writing it at Entumeni in Zululand when he was twenty-one and sent the manuscript to Leonard and Virginia Woolf at The Hogarth Press. Considering that it was written "with a hard pencil on thin paper, they must have had a strong curiosity to read it at all", as Plomer himself remarked many years later. But they did more than read it. They decided at once to publish it. A printers' strike delayed its appearance until the spring of 1926—a year which was to be full of fate for Plomer, two of his friends and his native South Africa.

In Britain and America the unusual quality of the book was recognized immediately. Plomer himself, in fact, found the American reviewers too generous to be convincing and wrote that he was already too well aware of his own limitations to have his head turned by finding great names in the same sentence as his own.[1] There was, however, at least one American comment which is well worth preserving: "Look elsewhere for your bedtime story", the *New York World* warned its readers.

Comment in Britain was more measured but perhaps all the more significant for that. Desmond MacCarthy, then at his best as a critic and reviewer, was the first to notice the

[1] *Double Lives*, an autobiography by William Plomer (Jonathan Cape.)

book in England. It had, he observed in the *New Statesman*, prevented him from looking out of a train window for at least three hours. The *Nation* called it "volcanic" and "although not what is usually called a great book, an important one". Another reputable writer said he was tempted to call it a work of genius though "he did not quite yield to the temptation", as Plomer again remarked with characteristic humour. Yet another reviewer called it "a book with a temperature" and one of Plomer's uncles wrote: "You have managed to catch an effect where tedious people only catch malaria", thereby demonstrating deftly in passing how natural and easy in the family were the wit and spirit of which his nephew had just delivered such startling proof.

How different the welcome in South Africa! Only three of the many newspapers and periodicals which hastened to review the book praised it and then mainly, perhaps, because the reviewers in question came from England and had had their values formed in the great mould of the European spirit to which Plomer himself ultimately belongs. Since the explosion which greeted *Turbott Wolfe* in South Africa was not a solitary and accidental event but really the first blast in a campaign which is yet far from over, these three reviewers merit a mention in this retarded despatch. One, Ruth Alexander, was the daughter of a Cambridge professor, the wife of a South African barrister and Liberal Member of Parliament, and a contributor to the *Cape Times*. She called it the most vital book about South Africa since *The Story of an African Farm*. Desmond Young, too, took up the cause in the *Natal Witness*, of which he had just become editor. His father, Commodore Sir Frederick Young, was the world's foremost salvage expert and as a young lad Desmond had been taken to the most remote and perilous foreshores of the world in the salvage steamer, *Ranger*. The trenches of Flanders had followed, and after that his whole life has been dedicated to adventure in the true meaning of the word: his flair in other dimensions of life told him immediately that *Turbott Wolfe* was authentic adventure of a kind South Africa had not experienced before. He committed his paper to an intelligent statement of his own intuitive perceptions; and characteristically, once committed, he never wavered. Finally there was Leonard Barnes, ex-Colonial Office and Rifle Regiment. Like Desmond Young, he had been decorated too for gallant conduct in the First World War and like many ex-officers he had been lured by the promises of politicians to invest all he had in a cotton scheme in Zululand where Plomer had written his novel. As the venture declined, he had fallen back more and more on writing, for which he had a considerable bent. He wrote a long, sensitive appreciation of *Turbott Wolfe* and largely as a result of writing it, joined Desmond Young in journalism, abandoned cotton planting for good, and quickly became a highly articulate power for enlightenment in the newspaper world of Southern Africa.

It is perhaps as true of books as of men that one can judge them by their enemies as well as by their friends. However vast their superiority in numbers, the people who attacked *Turbott Wolfe* in Africa never matched the quality of defenders like these. I myself have never forgotten the uproar which greeted the appearance of the book in South Africa and particularly in Natal where I was working. Apart from these three exceptions, all the English and Afrikaans newspapers and critics condemned the book in leading articles and bitter reviews. Supporting the angry editorials, the correspondence columns of the daily papers carried letters from "Mothers of Five", "Pro Bono Publicos" and so on and

INTRODUCTION

"Bookworm" moaned that *Turbott Wolfe* was "not cricket".

I remember the excitement and impassioned argument provoked at various times by *Lady Chatterley's Lover*, *The Well of Loneliness*, the publication in France of Claudel's correspondence with Gide over Gide's homosexuality; later, over the American nymphet *Lolita*, and recently over *Fanny Hill*. But none equalled the pitch and hysteria of this African occasion. I imagine one may well have to reach back to some aspects of the Dreyfus affair and Emile Zola for parallels, since the appearance of *Turbott Wolfe* had a marked sociological and political as well as a literary import. In fact, looking back on it all now, I find it something of a mystery that Plomer escaped the public tarring and feathering inflicted on a lecturer at a South African University some years later for far less said. However exaggerated the language may appear to a generation removed from the heat and dust of that day, Roy Campbell was not exaggerating the effect when he wrote in *The Wayzgoose* his satire on the people and events of that period.

> Plomer, 'twas you who, though a boy in age,
> Awoke a sleepy continent to rage,
> Who dared alone to thrash a craven race
> And hold a mirror to its dirty face.

One could have added also to this the observation of the master satirist, Dean Swift, "When a true genius appears in the World, you may know him by this sign, that the Dunces are all in confederacy against him."

Yet if one were to leave to the satirists alone the interpretation of the hullaballoo over *Turbott Wolfe* in Africa, one would miss much of its significance. For as I see it the trouble with satire is that it over-simplifies reality. I know that the armoury of the human spirit is not complete without it, and used as it is in Shakespeare, as one in a great and complex number of elements for capturing our imagination, I can relish it. But where it becomes the one and only weapon I have reservations. The satirist seems to me to have a tendency to abstract both himself and his theme from their human context. He presumes himself to be immune to the ailments of his time, ignores both his participation in the human condition and his own contribution to its inadequacy. He tends to set himself higher than the gods on Olympus who were continually and forever, despite their own immortal existence, involved in the mortal lot. From somewhere above heart and mind, preferring summary judgment and rough justice to slow understanding and compassion, the satirist is inclined to release on the societies and persons who have dismayed and hurt him such cold avalanches of retribution and correction that they chill me. In the purely satirical role he is incapable of melting the frost and ice within himself as Othello did by realizing, "The pity of it, Oh! Iago, the pity of it." The pity the satirist knows best is, perhaps, a pity for his own hurt self, even where it is most widely projected and disguised as a universal and objective concern over man's inhumanity to man.

In all the many issues and considerations brought to light in my native country by the publication of *Turbott Wolfe*, it was precisely "the pity of it all", and the incapacity of human beings to perceive it before rather than after the event, which seemed to me the most significant. If, as Campbell implied, the race had been more craven and its face dirtier than the fallible human norm, or had there been only dunces arrayed against Plomer, that could have been accepted by me. But unfortunately the villains of our daily round are neither Gullivers' giants nor even his pygmies. Our greatest enemies are too humanly normal and no more subtle than ourselves. We are all condemned to be the flies in our own ointment. On this occasion the "craven race" involved was all of us, working no less hard at keeping our face and hands clean and being neither less intelligent nor more stupid than the rest. Knowing the African story as I did in the bone and blood of a family which, on my mother's side, had been there since the European beginning nearly three hundred years before, there was enough of the good in it for me to believe salvation both possible and worth while. But the irony of the processes of abstraction, magnification and over-simplification of what I call the satirical fallacy in a curious way aided and abetted the ills they ostensibly set out to cure. They inclined to strengthen the chain of action and reaction which bound life to one inadequate expression of itself instead of freeing it for renewal.

In the same way I believe the world to-day is an accessory after the fact of the crime it condemns in South Africa, because of the lack of fullness in the pre-suppositions on which it bases its policies. Then, as now, the disconcerting heart of the matter was how my countrymen, so manifestly human and anxious to be decent, could not only tolerate but create conditions in their world which belied all these qualities, and round so savagely on a work like *Turbott Wolfe* which could only enlarge the values of the civilization of which they claimed, with passion, to be the only defenders in Africa. What perturbed me then, as now, was the spectacle of so much decency mobilized so easily overnight in a spirit so alien to itself, and consequently neither for the first nor the last time I found myself deeply involved in a kind of civil war. Plomer says he was told of a case where two men came to blows over his novel in a South African street. I came to blows over it in other ways with numbers of people, some of whom were my close friends, and soon found myself embroiled in a serious quarrel which reveals clearly the nature of the resistances to be faced by anyone who confronts an established order with the implication of his own increased awareness of reality. This quarrel was with Wodson, the editor of the newspaper on which I was working (the *Natal Advertiser*, which was to grow into the highly successful *Daily News* of to-day); he was one of the principal targets of Roy Campbell's scorn in *The Wayzgoose* and is referred to there as "Wod's Godson".

I owed Wodson much, for he was the only person in South Africa who had been prepared to employ me. On leaving school at the age of seventeen, and believing that the sooner I started writing the better, I had thought immediately, like many others before me, of newspaper work as the best preparation for such a career. Accordingly I had applied first to the up-and-coming Afrikaans newspapers of South Africa. Without exception they turned me down, the editor of the most illustrious of them all, *Die Burger*, informing me that he could not even consider employing a person who had not taken a university degree. I had turned then to the editor of the *Natal Advertiser* without much hope of success.

White Natal was almost entirely English-speaking. Durban prided itself on being the most English town in Africa. Both city and province were profoundly anti-Afrikaans and particularly resentful of the first Nationalist Afrikaner government which Hertzog had just led to power against their idol Smuts. Very few people in Durban spoke Afrikaans, although it was, with English, an official language of the land. It was scornfully dismissed as "kitchen dialect", a decadent form of Dutch, and one of the many inferior things that characterized the boorish Boers of the interior. Although an important element of the population of Durban made a good deal of money by selling the wool sent to them from the interior, they were incapable even of corresponding with their clients in Afrikaans, and I was for some years to add considerably to my small salary by translating letters to and from their customers. All people of Natal who could afford it sent their children to public schools and universities in England. They always talked of Britain as "home", even those who had never been there—and they were ninety per cent of the population.

To-day I find this rather touching, but then it infuriated me and set the seal on the misgivings I had of getting employment in such a community. To my amazement the editor of the *Natal Advertiser*, Harold Wodson, after talking to me for two hours, suddenly said in a voice that still had a strong Yorkshire accent: "You know, I rather like the idea of a young boy from the backveld working on an English newspaper. Mind, you'll be the only one. We are all English and English-born on this staff, except for one Durban lad. The main point is, can you write English well enough?" To prove it I went back to my hotel and wrote a piece on the "Superstition of Examinations in South Africa". Wodson not only gave me the job as a result but also published the piece in his newspaper. Months later his senior sub-editor confessed that there had nearly been a mutiny on the staff when they learnt the editor had decided to employ a backveld boy.

All this, I submit, shows that Wodson, far from being either "craven" or a "dunce", was a person of courage and active imagination. Moreover he was a man of liberal if somewhat old-fashioned views. He sat daily working at a desk which stood underneath an enlarged portrait of the great Scott of the *Manchester Guardian*. His profession to him was not just a means of broadcasting news but an honoured branch of literature. He loved books; Coleridge's *Biographia Literaria* was his Bible, Turner his favourite painter and Ruskin the one and only prophet of Art. In the course of many lessons he gave me on the law of libel he discussed at length the action Whistler had brought against Ruskin and remarked more than once how sad it was that Ruskin, who had been so right about Turner, could go so wrong about Whistler. I was not experienced enough to suspect what I now believe to be often true: that the faults we are most aware of in others are those of which we are unconscious in ourselves. Otherwise I might have had an inkling that Wodson himself was perhaps one day to be guilty of a Ruskin-Whistler error.

Nevertheless it was this blinkering of human perception that, to an important extent, accounted for the intellectual riot sparked off by the appearance of *Turbott Wolfe* in South Africa. Leon Daudet, the son of the great Alphonse whose work is undeservedly rejected to-day because of his own Ruskin-Whistler errors in the political life of France, argued with effect in two remarkable books, *L'Avenir de l'Intelligence* and *La Stupide XIXeme Siècle*, that much of what was wrong with nineteenth-century France was due to a hubris of the intelligence so great that it amounted to a form of stupidity and a blindness to what St Paul would have called "the evidence of things not yet seen". There was a good deal of this form of hubris about on the 1926 South African scene. The first intimation I had that my editor's great Ruskin-Whistler moment was upon him was when he summoned me early one morning, threw a book at me as if it stung between his fingers and commanded, "Read that and tell me what the modern world is coming to! I have just written my leader about it."

It was *Turbott Wolfe*, of course, and that evening I read a whole column of prose (not unworthy of Ruskin himself) leading to the conclusion that the world of Plomer's book was one "of shattered perspectives and perverse stimuli, of lascivious gods and outer darkness". At the time those resounding phrases did not convey to me any precise intellectual image so much as a discharge of feelings of disapproval almost too violent to be endured. To-day they are no clearer; but as the sound of wind among dry leaves or the smell of a wood-fire at sunset can instantly recall for me a long-vanished African experience, so they have the power to bring alive most painfully the bewilderment and dismay that I felt that night over my editor's reaction. I was barely nineteen at the time. Yet I could not put *Turbott Wolfe* down until I had read it from cover to cover. This establishment of a difference between Wodson and me was never erased, though we remained friends until his death. Almost daily we quarrelled over the book and inevitably all sorts of other latent differences were drawn to the issue. I found it in a very real sense a book of revelation. Art, to me, is a magic mirror wherein suddenly are made visible aspects of reality hitherto invisible, and this *Turbott Wolfe* was for me and some of my generation in South Africa. For my editor and his contemporaries, no matter how we argued and pleaded, it remained a work of total darkness. They would not even give it the conditional admission to their understanding that Calvin gave the Book of Revelation, with the fearsome proviso that though divinely inspired it was also "a dark and dangerously obscure book". Within a few months our differences had grown so acute that I was writing letters under my own name disagreeing with Wodson and his literary critic in the columns of the *Natal Advertiser* and he was answering back in his leading articles! And both the fact that he allowed this and could take this particular issue so seriously seems to me to-day considerably to his credit.

Inevitably there came a day of climax. For some time Roy Campbell had been pressing me to leave the newspaper and join him and Plomer on the south coast of Natal to work on the literary magazine they had started, *Voorslag*—the name was Afrikaans for the lash of a whip—of which I had already become a sort of Afrikaans editor, and at the same time to pursue my own writing. Disinclined to face another scene with Wodson after work, I wrote out a letter of resignation and placed it on his desk for him to read first thing the following morning. For the last time, as I thought, I turned to close the door on the beard of the great Scott in the portrait over the desk. Early the next morning I set out by municipal tram for the railway station to catch the one and only daily train to join Campbell and Plomer. On the way to town the tram was derailed and as a result I missed the train. Since the railway station was close to my newspaper office I decided to call in there in case any letters had arrived for me overnight. There was only one, and that from Campbell, informing me of a crisis in the affairs of *Voorslag* which might force him to resign and requesting me, for that and various other reasons, to hold on to my newspaper work for the moment. I retrieved my letter of resignation from the editor's desk only five minutes before he arrived and held on to my job with the *Natal Advertiser* as Roy had requested me to do, while *Voorslag* went through a stormy passage.

Looking back, it seems an odd series of what we call co-incidences. Yet the ancient Chinese believed that coincidences are not accidental but manifestations of a profound law of life of which we are inadequately aware. They hold that Time possesses a character of its own which colours what happens at any given moment anywhere in the world. This, they maintain, we dismiss as "sheer coincidence". The German conception of "Zeitgeist" is, I expect, the nearest European parallel and more acceptable to our normal way of thinking. I can only say in support of the Chinese belief that I have noticed that, when one renounces an established order and the protection of prescribed patterns of behaviour and, out of a longing for new meaning, commits oneself to an uncertain future like a fish to the sea, then "coincidences" crowd fast in on one like the salvoes of stars shooting out of the night in Southern Africa towards the close of the year. Coincidences, at these times, do not appear capricious and extraneous, but rather signs of confirmation that one has found again the rhythm and swing of the authentic sea of life.

All this, I think, shows what sort of an impact *Turbott Wolfe* had for me on all levels of life. For a start it brought me and Plomer together, and through Plomer I met Roy Campbell. For the first time in my life, instead of reading about literature in books, I was to be in intimate touch with its act of creation. Far more important, I was in touch with it through the work of contemporaries—Plomer was three years older than I was; Campbell a year or two older than Plomer. However much one can learn from the old and the experienced, there is nothing comparable to the dynamics of learning from people of one's own time, themselves caught up and struggling in the baffling process of expressing immediate apprehensions of a common reality. I could hardly have done without the companionship of mind and interests which Plomer and Campbell gave me, nor their example of how to set about the difficult business of self-employment as a writer. Consequently my debt to the two of them is immense. The debt of South Africa was to be even greater.

Campbell and Plomer were persons of profoundly different temperaments, gifts and tastes. Campbell's greatest gifts were romantic and Dionysian. He was naturally a wild person in the way that Africa was wild and brilliant before we spoiled and dulled it. His talent was impetuous from birth, flashing out of the dark without forewarning like a meteor to vanish without premonition into the night. It was perhaps a secret intimation of this that made him write in *Tristan da Cunha*,

> *over the wave*
> *Our ways divide, and yours is straight and endless*
> *But mine is short and crooked to the grave.*

He was unpredictable and ran easily to extremes. In his satires I knew all the characters, yet I could barely recognize the originals for the excess of caricature. I know Campbell too came to regret the extremes of his *Wayzgoose* mood and in time he swung right over to the other extreme. In his address to the University of Natal when many years later it conferred a doctorate on him, and not long before he died in a car accident in Portugal, he spoke, perhaps out of unconscious remorse, almost like a disciple of Dr Verwoerd. And this was as foreign to his real poetic self as had been the exaggerated accent of the satirist of the *Turbott Wolfe* period. Plomer's talent is classical and Apollonian, in love with proportion and the art of shaping and containing the shapeless and uncontained. Instinctively and inevitably his talent was committed to the increase of civilization, and charged to remain when the wild and the wilderness had been swept away and the hunter gone.

INTRODUCTION

But for a brief moment, as a result of this affair and the sense of crisis it produced in the imaginations of both men, the romantic and the classical were joined to defend something greater than either—as they could always be if only life were perfect and our daily portion of reality not so small and obstinately asymmetrical. The effect on Campbell's work in particular was remarkable. In the short while during which Plomer lived with him and his beautiful wife Mary at Sezela near Umdoni Park on the South Coast of Natal, he wrote, apart from much of *Voorslag*, some of his best poetry—much of it on themes that he would never have observed, I believe, had it not been for *Turbott Wolfe* and his association with Plomer. I think in particular of poems like "The Serf", "The Zulu Girl", and "Tristan da Cunha". Campbell himself was aware of this, and scattered throughout his work are typically large tributes to Plomer, as in the piece I have already quoted from *The Wayzgoose*, or the one wherein he speaks of the two of them as "Twin Sebastians/Each in his uniform of darts". Plomer himself was not, I guess, quite as obviously or deeply influenced, for it is in the nature of the classical to be more self-contained than the romantic. Yet he too, working as hard as Campbell did, among several remarkable pieces written at this time also composed "Ula Masondo", one of the truly great stories of our time.

I, who had come to spend my weekends with them, never ceased to marvel at the way they worked. I would leave Durban after the paper had been put to bed at about seven o'clock on a Saturday night, in a train that took me to within some miles of the bungalow wherein they lived. There the surf of the Indian Ocean was always pounding those yellow sands with an ancient Homeric urgency. A young Indian boy would meet me at about ten and together we would follow the railway line through dunes and tangled bush towards Sezela. Sometimes we had a moon so bright that I could almost read the headlines of the newspaper I carried with me. Sometimes it was so dark that the world lost all its shape and I could not have seen the sleepers at my feet had it not been for the hurricane lamp the young Indian always had with him because, he confided in me, of the leopards and other unspecified wild animals which he alleged still infested the bush beyond the dunes. I would arrive towards midnight fully expecting the household to be asleep, but always the three of them would be there still writing, talking, or reading aloud to one another by lamp and candle-light anything of interest they had discovered in the course of the day. I had thought we worked hard enough on my newspaper, particularly on Saturdays, but by then most of my colleagues would be rounding off some hours of drinking in their favourite pubs or fast asleep in bed. All Sunday while these workers of the world were at golf, cricket, tennis or Sabbath feasting, at Sezela the writing, reading and this related talk went on, and I would depart on Sunday night or early Monday morning leaving them still hard at it.

For me it was as if in the wilderness I had suddenly stumbled on a power house of the spirit and the bungalow was vibrating not with the shock of Vasco da Gama's sea so much as with a swiftly operating dynamo. The first time I went down to Sezela, Campbell and I talked for two nights and a day. Plomer and Mary Campbell knew the secret and the vital importance of the law of conservation of energy. They not only practised it but tried hard to conserve Campbell's energies for him. He learned more from them of self-discipline than he ever did from anyone else, but even that was not much. Born on fire, it was as if his whole being had already irrevocably accepted that he could only live by burning himself out. Sometimes after the others had gone to bed he and I would walk up and down the foreshore, the night restless with the quick, pointed stars—"tap dancers" as Campbell once called them to me—of our winter sky, and phosphorescent with that surf of thunder beside us. "Snore in the foam, snore in the spray, snore in the wind!" he would begin to declaim at the waves as if they were breaking on the rock of Tristan da Cunha itself, the South Atlantic island about which he had just written the first draft of his poem and of which these words were the opening line. Or he would recite from his favourite French poets who were closer to him than any others, such as Tristan Corbière, of whom there is a distinct echo in the lines just quoted, Baudelaire, whose "Albatross" he was translating, Villon, Valéry, Rimbaud, above all from the Bateau Ivre, even the arch-formalist Herédia. Sometimes while doing this he would be carrying in his arms his daughter Anna, a baby who cried a great deal at night just then, so that Mary, who bore an immense burden in that household, could have a good night's rest. Whenever Anna became restless Campbell would try to soothe her by singing sea shanties like "Shenandoah" to her or, if that failed, by making fires for her. She loved fires: one particularly bad night we started in a high wind such a fire that we came near to burning down one of the sugar plantations of Lewis Reynolds, the rich young man who financed *Voorslag*. After such an experience I would have expected Campbell, who looked unusually frail then, to rest the next day, but he joined in the round of the new day's activity as if he had slept all through the night.

Important to me too at the time was the daily demonstration implicit in their way of living that if one waited for a favourable environment and special conditions for writing one would never write at all. Their example taught me that the only way, no matter how discouraging one's surroundings, was to take up pen and paper daily and write. Mary Campbell worked wonders making the bungalow comfortable, but it had been built for quick extrovert weekends by the sea and not for permanent occupation, least of all by hard-working artists. Moreover, Campbell was a person of such profoundly impulsive and unpredictable nature that he could annihilate any routine or system of order however great. Yet the work seemed to pour out of them without apparent impediment.

So it went on until the final Sunday after my abortive attempt to quit my newspaper. That day three men appeared soon after breakfast: Lewis Reynolds, the sponsor of *Voorslag*; Maurice Webb, its business manager, intellectually of keen Fabian extraction, a worshipper of George Bernard Shaw and another target of Campbell's savage satire; and *Voorslag*'s art critic, a painter of whose pictures Campbell was to write that they were full of:

> A '*Light that never was on Land or Sea*',
> *Nor, thank the Lord, is ever like to be!*

The second number of *Voorslag*, which had been bitterly criticized in the press all over the country, was more than the three of them could stomach, and they came to us with a proposal that Webb, whose claim to editorial ability lay solely in the fact that he edited a business directory in Durban, should become also a kind of managing editor above Campbell and Plomer. Believing that Plomer was the unwanted influence in Campbell's life and the main transgressor against the public sense of propriety, they insisted on seeing Campbell alone. The meeting took place out on a sand dune, with

Plomer, Mary and myself watching from a distance, drawn together by a sense of impending disaster.

Campbell, whose sole source of income was *Voorslag*, squatted on his heels in the native South African fashion, a brisk sea-breeze tugging at his beard, while the visitors sat on the sands in front of him. It was all over in a few minutes. I saw Campbell suddenly gesticulate with his hands like a Zulu orator, get up abruptly and walk over to us, while the three others turned away disconsolately. Paler than usual with anger and in a voice still shaken with emotion, Campbell said, "They want to put Webb in over us. I told Lewis straight, 'You yourself confided to me in the beginning that we must take care not to let *Voorslag* develop *Webb*-ed feet, now you want it to have a *Webb*-ed head. You have my resignation here and now.'" The next number of the magazine carried this brief announcement on its first page: "I have much pleasure in announcing my resignation from *Voorslag*: Roy Campbell."

So, finally, *Voorslag* came to an end and within a few days Plomer and I found ourselves going to Japan as the result of a small service that I had been able to do for two distinguished Japanese journalists on their visit to S. Africa a few months back. I remained in Japan for a short time, but Plomer stayed on to write some of the most revealing stories ever written by a foreigner about the Japanese people. I returned to S. Africa to another year of rapidly growing differences not only with my newspaper but my own countrymen, started anew by another book of Plomer's, *I Speak of Africa*, which caused an even greater uproar than its predecessor. I felt singularly alone now, for Campbell in the meantime had gone with his wife and children to England. For Campbell and Plomer it was the end of what I call "the *Turbott Wolfe* period". For me the period was still to last a while longer like a bitter hang-over after too sweet an intoxication. But how prodigious the impact of the two men had been can be judged by the fact that, though we had all three been together barely four months, it still seems an age to me.

So much then for examples from my own experience of the effect and by-products of *Turbott Wolfe*. There remains, however, the most important matter of all: what was it in the book itself that could render it capable of influencing my generation so profoundly and of having consequences so far beyond the fields of art and literature? What indeed were these consequences and how far did they reach? The explanation, I believe, is centred in the fact that *Turbott Wolfe* was a book of revelation to us.

Consider for a moment what appear to me to be the four distinct phases of English literature in South Africa. The first begins with the appearance on our scene among the 1820 Settlers of a crippled Scot, Thomas Pringle. It is true there was the talented and charming Lady Anne Barnard, a daughter of the gifted house of Crawford and Balcarres and author of the ballad "Auld Robin Gray", whose letters from the Cape written some twenty years before Pringle have a technical claim to be called the beginning. But I overlook these because they might have been written anywhere in the world, their local colour going no deeper than the colour of its surroundings into a chameleon. But in the six years that he spent in Africa Pringle took the nature and the problems of the country deeply upon himself: he took the blow as it were not over the head but in the solar plexus of his sensitive, imaginative and courageous nature, and as a result left us a record in prose and verse of his single-handed encounter with South Africa. He wrote among other things a poem which

Coleridge himself described as "among the two or three most perfect lyric poems in our language". For all that, no matter how closely his wide-open nature enabled him to identify himself with the country, Pringle remained a foreigner writing about Africa in English.

The second phase comes with Olive Schreiner. With her, English literature in South Africa suddenly becomes profoundly indigenous and the imagination is native. She is utterly in and of the country, so much so that I have always believed that, had I been presented with an unknown piece of her writing, I would have been able to tell, just from its texture, that it had been written by someone born and raised in South Africa. As a very small girl she spent some years in the village in which I was born and to this day I see in the themes and the words she chose, this village and its surroundings prompting her wide, dreaming and prophetic soul. Indeed she expressed this, writing under the pseudonym of Ralph Iron, in her introduction to a new edition of *The Story of an African Farm*. She answered with these words the critics who would have liked her book "to be of wild adventure, of cattle driven into inaccessible kranses by Bushmen, of encounters with ravening lions and hair-breadth escapes. This could not be. Such works are best written in Piccadilly or in the Strand: there the gifts of the creative imagination, untrammelled by contact with any fact, may spread their wings. But, should one sit down to paint the scenes among which he has grown, he will find that the facts creep in upon him. Those brilliant phases and shapes which the imagination sees in far-off lands are not for him to portray. Sadly he must squeeze the colour from his brush, and dip into the grey pigments around him. He must paint what lies before him."

"Sadly he must squeeze the colour from his brush, and dip

into the grey pigments around him." That sentence alone is so stamped with the image of the Karoo where Olive Schreiner was born and lies buried that one could not fail to recognize it. And yet—great, good, imaginative and undeniably indigenous as she was—there is a curious limitation upon her awareness: the black and coloured people of Africa who were with her from birth and far outnumbered the white are not naturally and immediately in it. She too made her breakthrough but not in this direction. Her triumph was to realize for the first time the rejection of woman and her values in Africa in every except the purely biological sense. This was true not only of woman but far more subtly and profoundly true of those feminine aspects of man himself on which his capacity to be creative depends—I mean those aspects of the male imagination personified for Dante by Beatrice. It is, for instance, the accepting of his dependence upon them which explains the great role Beatrice plays in his *Divine Comedy* and the confidence with which he can face all the devils in Hell because, as he tells his guide, "Heaven has a noble lady who takes compassion on me." The point is fundamental to an understanding of Olive Schreiner's awareness, because the deep rejection of woman in our man's world proceeds directly from the failure of man to honour the woman in himself.

One reason why the history of Africa is so terrible is that the lack of recognition and the scale of this rejection has been so great. Olive Schreiner seems to have known this with a clarity and precision that still seem miraculous and, of course, the moment she gave words to her feeling in *The Story of an African Farm*, the great world outside immediately recognized it because there was not a society on earth which was not guilty to some extent of the same rejection and aggressive narrowing of human awareness. Olive Schreiner's first book to me, therefore, is not a novel so much as a documentary of this rejection of woman and a painful inventory of all that men have so blindly taken from her throughout the ages. Absence of form and over-profusion of charged sentences in her work are all criticisms levelled at her to this day. But one might as well complain of the lack of symmetry and over-abundance of lines in an Admiralty chart of a dangerous sea. This sense of rejection remained an obsession to the end of her days, but she was great enough to let it lead her to feel deeply for all forms of rejection in life. She became increasingly aware, too, of the rejection of the black and coloured people of the land, but aware of it mainly as matter for her Protestant and missionary conscience. Her concern for the people was ethical, and they themselves were the raw material of a grave problem which she wanted solved with justice. As people in their own individual right, alas! they never walked in her imagination or understanding. And in that too she was truly indigenous. No wonder that, for all her concern and her great example, the African and coloured peoples remained as absent from our literature as the working classes of England from one of Jane Austen's novels.

The third phase, overlapping Olive Schreiner's in time, is that of Rider Haggard. Quite apart from the fact that he wrote stories of adventure which will be read as long as there are young people in the world, he was of great pioneering importance to us in Africa because he was the first to find the black man romantic. He did not do this at long range, from Europe. Haggard found the black man a subject of romance and wonder as a result of daily contact with him, and on a scale and with an intensity that no one had ever done before. He saw in the black man something epic and heroic, his spirit an instrument of honour in search of greater honour. To know human beings through the sense of wonder they provoke is, I believe, the beginning of grace on this earth. To continue in this wonder, despite one's increasing knowledge, and carry through with it to the end, is the true fulfilment of grace. Rider Haggard was the first pioneer of this kind in our national imagination, and I can still remember the acute sense of reassurance and liberation of my own childish feelings about the black people that I experienced when I first read him as a young boy. How great was his achievement in this respect can perhaps be best measured by the fact that even to-day most white people in South Africa are incapable of experiencing a sense of wonder about the black people. If only we could begin to wonder, to take them into the light and shelter of our living imagination, the barriers that divide us so sharply would soon crumble. But there remains this obstinate black-out in the minds of most white people in Africa, all the more sinister because it is unconscious and often present in the best and most lovable of people. But an appreciation of this lack of perception is vital to an understanding of what *Turbott Wolfe* meant to us.

The fourth phase is, of course, William Plomer. It is true Roy Campbell had already succeeded as no other poet before him in giving South African poetry a contemporary idiom, and achieved a world-wide reputation with his long poem, *The Flaming Terrapin*.—"Il procède de Marlowe et de Rimbaud", a French critic had recognized. But the particular increase and heightening of awareness, which is perhaps the artist's most important contribution to life, came only with Plomer. For the first time in our literature, with *Turbott Wolfe*, a writer takes on the whole of South African life. Suddenly the barriers are down and imagination at last keeps open house in a divided land. The black people of South Africa are no longer just a problem. "My good man," Mabel van der Horst, one of the key characters in *Turbott Wolfe*, observes to a parson, "there is no native question. It isn't a question. It's an answer." Nor, in *Turbott Wolfe*, are the black people used merely as an incitement to adventure and romance. They take their place in their own right as individual human beings beside the white persons in the story. Some people in Europe to-day might think that this was obvious enough; but forty years ago it was a pioneering achievement of courage and originality as great as any in our history.

This matter of courage in the exercise of imagination has received scant appreciation in the evaluations of literature. Nothing, indeed, is generally more taken for granted than the power of imagination in the artist. There is a popular opinion that imagination exists independently by some magic of spontaneous generation and, of its own volition, will do the work for writer and artist—an opinion the more deceptive by reason of its half-truth. The fact that it presents the artist among many other problems with dangers and fears, from which only courage of a high order can set him free, is rarely understood. Yet no one who tries to serve his imagination through his own apprehensions of reality, as opposed to accepting conventional and collective ones, is long left in doubt on this score. This surely is what Gerard Manley Hopkins meant when he wrote:

> *O the mind, mind has mountains; cliffs of fall*
> *Frightful, sheer, no-man-fathomed . . .*

Part of the vertigo to be overcome arises, naturally, from the conflict bound to arise between the particular and personal apprehensions to which I have referred and the conventional, established and profoundly conditioned nature of the collective attitude to life. It also arises from the nature of the world within the artist himself where the imagination, or, to borrow a phrase of Sidney Keyes', "the river mind", has its source. The first part of the proposition is obvious enough, the second needs elaboration.

In the main, people are apt to think that what they observe in the outer world is the only *objective* reality and what they experience inwardly is the only *subjective* reality. It has always seemed to me there is an inner objectivity equal and complementary to the outer: two great worlds to which the individual is jointly subject, both of which he experiences subjectively, and in the process discovers his own meaning only to the extent to which his experience serves him in making a bridge between the two. Manley Hopkins saw this so clearly that he formulated his own characteristic concept in order to report on the matter to his own generation. There were not only "landscapes", he informed his contemporaries, but "inscapes" as well. These "inscapes" had objective perils, difficulties and problems to be overcome as great as those that beset the human being in the world without.

The history of art and literature indeed contains as many examples of persons who have succumbed before the perils encountered in the world within as those who have been overcome by their difficulties in the world without. The asylums of the world are full of people who have been overwhelmed by what has welled up within them: instincts and intuitions shaped over aeons in which they had played no part, and imposed on them by life without their leave or knowledge. The person who enlists in the service of the imagination, as do the artist and writer, has continually to come to terms and make fresh peace with this inner aspect of reality before he can express his full self in the world without. Many are so appalled by the difficulties and terrifying implications of what they see within themselves that, after a few bursts of lyrical fire, they either retreat into the previously prepared positions conventionally provided for these occasions by their social establishments; or else they close up altogether or take to drink or commit suicide. Nor is there any comfort to be found in thinking that this kind of defeat is suffered only by the lesser breeds among artists and writers: there are too many distinguished casualties. There is, for instance, the uncomfortable example of Rimbaud who, though a poet of genius, found the implications of genius more than he could bear and took on the perils of gun-running in one of the most dangerous parts of Africa as a more attractive alternative. Yet before he turned a deaf ear to the profound voice of his natural calling, he had shaped a vision of reality which increased the range of poetry for good. One may regret his desertion, but surely no one who cares for poetry can read "Bateau Ivre" and "Les Illuminations", for example, without some understanding of the power of the temptation, and an inkling of how exposed and vulnerable the ordered personality is to the forces of this world that the artist carries within him.

The suicide of Van Gogh is another instance. We owe it to him that our senses are aware of the physical world in a way not previously possible (except perhaps by the long-forgotten child in all of us when the urgent vision is not yet tamed and imprisoned in the clichés of the adult world). But because of Van Gogh, cypresses, almond blossom, corn-fields, sunflowers, bridges, wicker chairs and even trains are seen through eyes made young and timeless again and our senses are recharged with the aboriginal wonder of things. Here was not only genius but also high courage. Yet nothing so well gives one the measure of these inner forces as the fact that they were able to destroy both courage and genius.

What adds to the difficulties, already formidable, of taking up a private and personal vision of reality is that, in the extent to which it is unique, there is no known way of proving it. The voice which summons the individual pledged to commit his individuality to life is imperative: but his own powers to do so are untried and suspected of being unequal to the enormity of the task demanded of them. He, in his private way, is faced with a universal and ever-recurring predicament best symbolized in the Old Testament story of Moses and the burning bush. Ordered by his vision to confront Pharaoh and demand the release of his people, Moses even though assured and reassured of the authenticity of the vision, feels he has not the power to serve it. He expresses his sense of powerlessness with such phrases as "I am not eloquent", "I am slow of speech and of slow tongue", or as the Dutch Bible in its forthright way puts it simply, "I stutter". So the person with a unique vision finds his senses bound to a despotic Egypt long established and fortified by custom and tradition, and the story of the journey through the Red Sea, the wandering, suffering, and doubting of the original vision in the desert are symbolic of what the artist must endure if his own particular promise is to be fulfilled and the terms of his own private contract with living life observed.

I do not know what went on in Plomer's mind before he took to writing. I have never discussed it with him. But he himself many years later writing in *Double Lives* of the moment when he began *Turbott Wolfe*, says, "I was full of youthful priggishness, of the conceit of the solitary and the false confidence of inexperience, and, in the matter of writing a novel, I was attempting to reach by a short-cut what can only become even visible by taking an arduous road."

I am afraid I have quarrelled with this sentence from the moment I first read it. Fortunately the human personality is so much more than any individual can ever formulate. Roy Campbell provides the most vivid illustration of this that I have ever encountered. He had never any adequate conscious conception of what he really was. If I had had to accept as true of his whole personality the inferior ideas he often championed, I would have despaired of him from the moment I met him. But as a person and as a poet he was something different—gentler, more lovable and far more meaningful than he or his reasoning ever knew.

Plomer was more self-aware than Campbell. This was inevitable because of the differences implicit in their respective gifts. The classical and Apollonian is always, I think, more analytical and conscious of its purpose than the romantic and Dionysian. Nobody, for instance, has been more critical of Plomer than Plomer himself. In fact I would be inclined to say that as an artist his conscious, analytical self has been perhaps too severe with the instinctive content and raw material of his spirit. I certainly do not recognize either the writer or the man I knew from the statement of his that I have just quoted. I never saw any traces of these characteristics in the boy sitting down to write his first book at a remote place in Zululand called Entumeni or "Place of Thorns". The judgment, to me, remains as harsh as it is incomplete. What Plomer calls "youthful priggishness", I found a natural impatience with the underlying hypocrisies of civilized life around him. The "conceit of the solitary" to which he refers, I preferred to call the confidence of someone whose courage had not failed him in dealing with the inner dangers and fears to which I have referred.

Later in his career, I must confess I have felt that after *Turbott Wolfe* and some of the superb stories like "Ula Masondo" which revolve around it like a full moon about its native earth, Plomer did recoil somewhat from the implications and natural consequences of such disturbing powers of vision in himself. I believe he was increasingly hard on the Turbott Wolfe aspect of himself and for years ceased to write about the Africa which he had seen with a clarity, and felt with a depth and precision that no one has excelled. I have always feared he might have inflicted a wound on himself in the process. Yet I could easily be wrong. He belonged after all also to Europe, particularly to England. Moreover, our journey to Japan and his years in that country presented him with experiences it would have been extremely wasteful to have denied; just as it would have been unnatural and impossible to reject the England in himself. Besides, Plomer is still writing and such judgments at the best can be only provisional. Who knows that when the work of a lifetime is finally completed the verdict may well be that he did right to step back from the Turbott Wolfe "inscape" because it enabled him to resume an advance on a far broader front than otherwise would have been possible. D. H. Lawrence wrote about his own youthful poetry:

> *All these pure things come foam and spray of the sea*
> *Of Darkness abundant: which shaken mysteriously*
> *Breaks into dazzle of living: as dolphins leap from the sea*
> *Of midnight and shake it to fire, till the flame of the shadow*
> *we see.*

(last stanza of "Blueness")

INTRODUCTION

Turbott Wolfe, "Ula Masondo", parts of *I Speak of Africa*, poems like "The Scorpion" are "dolphins" of this kind, and I find it significant that even forty years later, when he approaches the period in which he wrote his first book, this antique sea is shaken again and begins to break into "a dazzle of living". In one of his recent poems, "Bamboo", he draws on the experience of his Japanese period which came immediately after *Turbott Wolfe*. I find it remarkable how, as he penetrates deeper within himself, the pulse of the poet quickens, the eye brightens and the images, grey under the ashes of burnt-out years, are blown into flame again. No, this "conceit of the solitary" is for me another typically self-depreciating way of saying that he had made his stand and won his peace with his world within. *Double Lives*, too, makes it clear that there had been a time when being "solitary" had no compensation of "conceit" and the loneliness had been almost unendurable. And there is, perhaps, no loneliness greater than that of being a stranger in one's own home.

Plomer had been born in South Africa, but his earliest years were spent partly there and partly in England. His conscious tastes, interests and values were largely formed by an English education and the traditions of a family deeply rooted in the past of England. His work may show how important the first five years of his life were in his imagination, and prove a vindication of the Jesuit claim for the lasting importance of those years. He had almost nothing in common with the Africa to which he returned except his native sense of belonging. Even his father appeared estranged to him and for years did not understand him. After another brief period of schooling he was set to do things which were basically alien to him and a deviation from his natural line of development. These things are described in *Double Lives* and need no repetition here, except as evidence of isolation and great loneliness. "Had I not been so busy, the solitude might all the same have driven me mad or peculiar," he wrote of his apprenticeship to a farmer in the remote Stormberg or Mountain-of-Storm district of South Africa. "To speak paradoxically I felt strongly", he added later, "the constriction of the great open spaces," and finally, most revealing of all, "I was too much alone with my turbulent thoughts and there was nobody to tell them to. It may be true that it is only by being alone that a man (even an adolescent man) can find himself, but it is not by being alone that he can find his proper level."

He was destined to be alone in the sense most important to him, the man born to be a writer and poet, until his meeting with Campbell soon after the appearance of *Turbott Wolfe*. Nothing worth while, Goethe wrote, has ever emerged from man without being tested first in loneliness and isolation. *Turbott Wolfe* was tested to the full in this way before it saw the light of day. The hero of the novel is a man who is desperately lonely, and he could have been conceived only in an imagination which had come to terms with its own isolation with success. To use Rilke's great remark, *Turbott Wolfe* was the work of someone who had succeeded in making "loneliness his home". How deeply in the process he had looked over "the cliffs of fall" into the deeps "no-man-fathomed", is clearest perhaps for me in two lines from one of the three poems in the book:

> *Fear has withered swiftly since*
> *HORROR was written on the sun.*

But most misleading of all in the quotation from *Double Lives* is the following. "In the matter of writing a novel, I was attempting to reach by a short-cut what can only become even visible by taking an arduous road." *Turbott Wolfe* was no short cut. It was the beginning of a process of growth so native that I personally do not believe Plomer ever saw farther or more deeply than he did then.

At another level, no less remarkable was the steadfastness with which Plomer maintained his own untried view of the life around him against that taken for granted by the European community of South Africa. The attitude of white South Africans to their coloured and black countrymen had never before been challenged in depth from their own midst. It had been challenged repeatedly from Europe and white South Africans had long since developed their own immunities to criticism from abroad. They could in any case always claim, not without justice, that their foreign critics neither knew their problem nor had to live its answer, and that being high-minded in the lives of others was a classical way of evading the discomforts of a conscience failing to face up to its own shortcomings. In so far as there had been a challenge in their own country, it had been uttered in such a rational, idealistic and cerebral manner that it had never provoked any of the great passion and emotion which, along with all persons of colour, had been locked away in a grim underworld of the national spirit. Challenges of this kind reached only the surface dimension of the racial problem: the levels on which it was envisaged were historical, geographical or economic. But that it was also a problem on a far deeper level, that it was a product of the unawareness of the European himself, of the hypocrisy, narrowness and blindness with which he led his own life, and that somewhere in the deeps of his nature this terrible denial of his own other self had been projected on to the despairing and rejected coloured peoples of the land, this had never before been presented in such a way. Further, the one had become the symbol of the other so that the suppression of one seemed dependent on the subjugation of the other and ultimately the reason why the white South African could neither perceive nor accept the common humanity of the black was just because it would mean that he would have to face his own inferior self within and begin a painful scrutiny of himself and his most cherished values.

White African awareness, of course, was aggravated increasingly by the Calvinism my countrymen had evolved for themselves in Africa. It was ironic that this kind of religion had the most irreligious consequences and affected the attitude of the average white South African to his coloured neighbours. The particular damage done by Calvinism to the totality of the human spirit is that it has raised the cold, rational, argumentative aspects into a tyranny over the warm, instinctive, intuitive and natural man. The Calvinist, particularly in South Africa, tends to be a depressingly literal person almost incapable of grasping the underlying symbolism of life and meaning. Some years ago a distinguished South African theologian was tried for heresy because he had taught that the Bible was not purely a history of literal truth but history transformed to give a symbolic and allegoric presentation of reality. I was present at the trial and I asked one of his judges, "Uncle, do you really believe that Jonah was swallowed by a great fish and after three days spat out on the shores of Nineveh?"

"Cousin," he replied, "if the Bible told me Jonah had swallowed the great fish, I would take it to have been so."

Magnificent in a way, but hardly the whole truth, and valuable only as a measure of how great is the incapacity of the European in Southern Africa to grasp a symbolic presentation of reality. I think, in fact, that what was a legitimate reaction at the time of the Reformation against a legacy of over-introspection from the Middle Ages, has now developed a hubris of its own and become this incapacity in modern man to experience meaning naturally and symbolically. And this hubris is the main reason why colour prejudice is much greater in Protestant than in Catholic countries. In Italy, where the spiritual lines of communications with the pre-Reformation world are most intact, I find it impossible to make my Italian friends understand colour-prejudice. I am not a Roman Catholic, but I would be a fool to ignore that in Catholic cultures colour prejudice is either non-existent or appears in a form far less virulent than in Protestant ones. This I believe is due to the Catholic respect for the symbolic nature of reality and hence its far greater tolerance of natural man. It seems to me that the kind of Calvinist society into which I was born in South Africa hated natural man not only because the Calvinist hated him in himself but because he was secretly attracted to him; and sensed that he might be in danger of abandoning the conscious, argumentative, dutiful, self-justifying, time-conscious, joyless hypocrite he had unconsciously become. In brief he feared that, if not daily on his guard, he himself might go "black" in the sense that black was the image of all that was natural and rejected in himself.

There are these and so many other similar and complex considerations that I once wrote a book about them,[1] for their effects seemed to charge the European spirit in Africa with passion. Norman Leys' book, *Kenya*, on settler beginnings in Kenya, aroused such outcries in 1926 that a man who had obtained a copy in secret brought it wrapped in a travelling rug for me to read as he was afraid of what might happen were he seen with it! Since then, although basically the same,

[1] *Dark Eye in Africa.*

these passions have become more sophisticated and subtler. Their intolerance has discovered a use even for tolerance; the passions, as the closely argued and highly orchestrated policy of apartheid in South Africa shows, are far better rationalized to-day. But *Turbott Wolfe* caught them unprepared. There was nothing to protect the community from the book's effects. It could not explain Plomer away as a foreigner who knew his facts from afar. He had been born into them, and had served a gruelling apprenticeship in various walks of life and in far more parts of the country than the average South African saw in a lifetime. He had taken the trouble to do what very few of them do even to this day: he had learned a Bantu language. Here clearly was an authentic challenge, presented in the vital dimensions up to then ignored in the European reckoning. It could not be dismissed as propaganda of any kind; it expounded no theories; it was not an appeal to conscience nor a moral tract. It was something before and beyond all these things: the work of an artist whose interest fundamentally was in people for what they were in themselves and what, in the midst of their troubled, confused, brittle and inadequate being, they were in the process of becoming. Only a person who has grasped the symbolic nature of life, the dream texture of reality, and recognized the urgent world within himself seeking flesh and blood to live in the world without, can take such a view and stake all on understanding rather than judgment. Nadine Gordimer some years ago grasped the importance of this: "William Plomer and Olive Schreiner," she said, "seize upon and decode these symbols that even in our dreams disguise from us our deepest selves." I would beg leave only to make one amendment to that pregnant observation and say, "these symbols that in our dreams inform us of our deepest selves".

INTRODUCTION

The supreme example of an artist aware of the symbolic nature of life was, of course, Shakespeare, who knew "the prophetic soul of the wide world dreaming on things to come". In that soul there is continual understanding, and a judgment and justice so unadventitious that not even all the villainy of Iago could make Shakespeare lose respect for the curious validity of his twisted character. This understanding, aware not only of things as they are but also as they will become, is present to a remarkable degree in the young writer of *Turbott Wolfe*. It is true that there are asides and barbed remarks that came at times from the hurt man rather than the writer of the novel. But on the whole it remains an exceptionally unbiased, rounded and unsentimental view of reality. This view was so natural and immediate that it confronted all that was artificial and calculated for social effect in our national character like a clear mirror suddenly held up in front of a human being who had never seen his face before. One can imagine with what result.

As children in Africa we used to place a mirror before the baboons we had captured. The baboons would find their own reflection incredible. They were convinced that the features belonged to another baboon and not themselves. They would search frantically at the back of the mirror for the other baboon and of course could not find him. Yet whenever they returned to the glass there was an authentic baboon-person staring back at them. But no matter how long this went on they could never accept that the reflection was their own. In their highly neurotic and intelligent way they were convinced that a dirty trick was being played on them, and the exercise would end with them picking up the mirror and smashing it to pieces. This has always seemed to me a precise rendering of South Africa's reaction to *Turbott Wolfe*.

Here are a few examples of the things that South Africa found intolerable in the book. Turbott Wolfe, the main character in the novel, found great beauty among the black people. He gives us the excitement one feels in discovering the idiom of beauty of another race and colour. In this crossing of the frontier of conventional attitudes and social taboos, one's sense of liberation was immense. The Bushman in the Kalahari say that their great first spirit not only gave things their names but their colours as well, applying them with variously coloured honeys. This was their natural and symbolic way of saying that giving life different colours was a sweet thing to do. Yet the child in South Africa had been educated out of this natural reaction and taught to think of the black people as ugly. One of the things I remember most clearly from my past was the common reference to black people as "ugly creatures". But in the deeps which *Turbott Wolfe* stirred, of course, it was another matter.

Finally, in *Turbott Wolfe* the hero found one Zulu girl so beautiful that he fell in love with her. That, of course, roused an even angrier reaction from the white South Africans. One of the cardinal principles of the popular attitude was that it was impossible for a decent, civilized white man to be attracted by black women. Only the decadent and the depraved could be capable of such a thing. This was one of the crucial hypocrisies of European life in South Africa; the existence of the talented and lovable coloured population of the Cape is proof of both the hypocrisy and the attraction so openly and sensitively described by Plomer. Indeed this story of Turbott Wolfe's love for the Zulu girl is one of the most moving things in the book and a wonderful example of the classical approach to a romantic theme. Here too is evident Plomer's capacity for investing the people and things of the physical world with abiding symbolism. Scene after scene is described with sensitivity and concentration of feeling, as if the thin skin had been stripped from the artist, the nerves exposed and the raw flesh in direct contact with life. Nor is this Zulu girl just an object of desire for Turbott Wolfe. "She was," Turbott Wolfe says, "an ambassadress of all that beauty, it might be called holiness, that intensity of the old wonderful unknown primitive African life outside history, outside time, outside science. She was a living image of what has been killed by people like Flesher (a European in the book), by our obscene civilization that conquers everything."

And Turbott Wolfe, in his self-defeated love of this woman through whose beauty not only the past but also the future of Africa beckons, is a moving symbol of the civilization he calls "obscene". He can recognize what is sterile and destructive in his civilized values, he can be stirred by the beauty of Africa, yet he is just as incapable of rejecting the one as committing himself to the other. He expresses in his own life the failure of an important aspect of civilization in Africa, so much so that when he lies dying one feels an entire epoch is perishing with him. In the book he knows that he is dying and says so to the narrator, who then remarks, "Turbott Wolfe paused. I could hear the thudding of a football being kicked and vague shouts that filled the winter afternoon. And in that sad and slovenly room I felt very vividly the state of this man who had been torn with so many sharp emotions, true or false, and who seemed, perhaps, because of them to belong utterly to a country of calm suns and plumy flowers. The window-curtains in that room were strewn with patterned faded poppies that moved, nodding maliciously, as the curtains moved, promising an anodyne; waiting, heavy budded, for a time when the room should be empty and obscure. . . ." The quotation shows Plomer's uncanny ability to make even what is inanimate in the physical world express the movements and emotions of the spirit, and in it I see the sun going down over a whole period of history.

Yet all is not defeat in the book. There is one character, a white woman, Mabel van der Horst, who is capable of the commitment that Turbott Wolfe eschews and who actually marries a black man, both because she loves him and because she believes ultimately that it is the only answer to colour and racial prejudice. Among the many heresies in *Turbott Wolfe* this was, for white South Africa, the greatest of all. In a country where the most savage emotions could be roused and the most liberal spirit silenced by the single question, "Would you like to see your sister married to a nigger?" this was clearly unforgivable. All the latent passion, connected in the South African character with matters of colour, came alive and was reinforced by the immense pressures created by its bleak Calvinist inhibitions of sex. The uproar was violent and prolonged, yet the ground in the imagination had been ploughed and the seed sown, and the idea that such things were not only possible but could even be desirable was planted there openly for the first time in our contemporary history.

Turbott Wolfe has dated little. It was written nearly forty years ago and I had expected to find signs of real wear and tear in the tale. Yet basically there is none. Its original validity is intact. Its age shows only in externals which serve in the end to reinforce the prophetic undertones of the story. For instance, when *Turbott Wolfe* was written there was no law in South Africa against marriage between white and black, so Mabel van der Horst's marriage to a Zulu was entirely possible. Here is evidence enough of the decline foretold in the story. To-day, not only is marriage legally impossible but even casual sexual intercourse between white and black is a criminal offence, subject to the most severe penalties. The props and the costumes in the theatre may have changed, but the characters and the play are the same. Indeed it is remarkable how their equivalents still walk the scene: the Scandinavian and other missionaries of *Turbott Wolfe* are still there; so are men like Turbott Wolfe, capable of recognizing the challenge to civilization but incapable of taking it up; so are respectable Europeans lusting at heart after experiences that their respectability vociferously condemns. Bantu servant girls with the air of Empresses waiting on faded gentility (refugees now from English income tax rather than escapers from a cramped Victorian world); priests baffled and defeated by life forces as unchristian as they are unmanageable; political parsons who believe not so much in making politics Christian as turning Christianity political; and most in evidence of all is the equivalent of the half-educated African, whom Turbott Wolfe finds weeping outside his window in the moonlight because he can never return to the tribal pattern from which he has been wrenched, yet is not allowed to enter the world for which his education has been the preparation. These and many more key figures of the African world are sketched into this novel. And perhaps most prophetic of all, the Communist agent, he is called "Bolshevik" by Plomer, and the immense potential of Russian influence in Africa, are important elements in the story. Considering that when *Turbott Wolfe* was written the Revolution in Russia was barely seven years old, the country ruined by civil war, disease and famine and its power in the world negligible, I find this an impressive example of visionary writing.

Among all these characters sketched so vividly in *Turbott*

Wolfe, there is only one that is not on the South African stage to-day. That she is now somewhere in the wings and ready to walk on I have no doubt, but at the time when I first read *Turbott Wolfe* I doubted it strongly. At the time it seemed to me that, if there were such a person as Mabel van der Horst, she would be least likely to be found among my Afrikaner countrymen, because the resistances I have described were most deeply entrenched in them. But I see her to-day as a clear image of an underlying factor in the South African tragedy. The Afrikaner rejects the black man because the black man so profoundly and secretly appeals to him. What passes for hatred is really fear of a greater love, and only people who see love as a protracted Technicolor kiss against a sunset can fail to realize that love implies disconcerting consequences and changes, in societies as well as individuals. This love, which every Afrikaner has known who has been nursed by coloured women and whose earliest companions were black children, may be suppressed in the adult but it remains there, like a strange magnet, beneath the surface. It explains why in South Africa the majority of personal relationships between individual white and black are so good, far better than in North America; and why even the direst supporters of Dr Verwoerd on the collective front go to enormous lengths to absorb the shock of apartheid for the coloured people they know and employ. This is still one of the many paradoxes of life in South Africa, and it is this ambivalence in the national character which, with remarkable insight, Mabel van der Horst is made to represent.

In this respect she links up too with the beginning of European literature about Africa. In the sixteenth century one of Europe's greatest poets, the Portuguese Camoens, sailed round the Cape of Good Hope in a convoy bound for the

Far East. On his return to Portugal he wrote an epic called *The Lusiad*, in which he describes the journey of Vasco da Gama, the discoverer of the route by way of the Cape of Good Hope to the Far East. At this time no Portuguese had landed at the Cape and penetrated to the interior where the black races were slowly advancing South. Yet Camoens tells how one calm clear evening off the Cape, Vasco da Gama, alone on deck, is over-awed by a sudden darkening of the sky. He looks up and sees a gigantic black shape with negroid features towering over his ship. This gigantic shape booms at him, "I am the spirit of this far-flung and much tormented[1] Cape." Camoens significantly returns to Bartholomew Diaz's description of it as "The Cape of Storms". The black shape explains that he is the last of the Titans, that he has dared to love a white nymph and daughter of the God of the Sea who had been promised to him because of the help he had given the Gods in their struggle against the Titans. When the battle was over she was denied him and his love of this nymph, white with foam and spray of the sea, was regarded as so grave a presumption that he was bound to the Cape and turned to stone. The black giant then tells Vasco da Gama that a day will come when the Portuguese will be called to account and severely punished for having broken so brutally into the remote worlds of the East. Here, in the form of a poetic intuition and parable, is the history of Africa. The black man received from the European many of the gifts resulting from his Roman virtues; but just as the Roman denied the Etruscan, so the black man was denied the white love of which Camoens' nymph is the image, and in the process his heart was turned to stone.

The same intuition in Plomer perceived and selected Mabel

[1] The Portuguese word for storm is "tormentos".

van der Horst and made of her marriage to a Zulu a prophetic image: a union of spirit in which white love will no longer be denied to black Africa. And who can say to-day, more than four centuries after Camoens' poem was written, that the moment of reckoning it foretold has not come? The European Empire in the Far East and Africa is fast dissolving. For me in South Africa the day of reckoning started with *Turbott Wolfe*. It ended the age of European innocence in Africa. Before then all our faults and injuries to Africa could be forgiven because we were a civilization and a people who did not fully perceive what we were doing. But from the moment of *Turbott Wolfe*'s publication all those who dealt in the traffic of the spirit should have had their vision cleared. Apartheid, to me, is a truly horrible political expedient because it is evolved by a people who know it to be unworthy, and who merely exemplify man's capacity for finding good reasons for doing bad things.

As I see it, the beginning of all things is Euclidian, a point in the human spirit where the future has no magnitude or size but only position. In this novel the new era of reckoning not only has position but substance for the first time in our history. And once one individual has perceived a new vision of truth, and had the courage to express and assert it, life can never be quite the same again. For my part I have always looked for the origin of things at the point where the future first had position in the human imagination. When I had to write a report for the Foreign Office in 1947 about events in Indonesia, I started with the appearance of *Max Havelaar*, the great novel by Geeraard Douws Dekker, who wrote under the pseudonym of Multatuli, the Latin for "I Have Suffered Much". This novel erupted into the nineteenth-century awareness of Holland much as *Turbott Wolfe* did into that of

South Africa. It was, for me, the beginning of the end of Empire and the age of established social values.

My view was confirmed by my recent discovery in Russia of the importance that the Russian writers and intelligentsia had attached to this book. Like *Max Havelaar* in Holland and Indonesia, Plomer changed the course of our imagination in South Africa. To this day South African literature uses *Turbott Wolfe*, consciously or unconsciously, as a kind of compass. I noticed on my return from our journey to Japan as early as 1927 that, short as my absence had been, a subtle change had taken place in the intellectual climate of South Africa. Writers and journalists were thinking and saying things they could not have said before *Turbott Wolfe*. While we were in Japan General Hertzog, the leader of the reactionary Nationalist forces in South Africa, and his lieutenant Klasie Havenga, had returned from an Imperial Conference, waving the Statute of Westminster in their opponents' faces and announcing that South Africa was independent and free to follow its own history. Almost immediately the first colour legislation was passed by the Union Parliament and the Generals' policy of "segregation", the infant now grown into the giant apartheid, was enunciated. So, the vital mobilization of the oldest forces in the human spirit that fight the battle of renewal had begun; on one side those who wanted to conserve, on the other those working for change: on one side an organized and deeply entrenched social order; on the other the imponderable forces of the human imagination instructed by the symbolism of the wholeness of life and armed only with the energies at its disposal.

Not long before his death, at the time of our battle in South Africa against the scandalous and successful Nationalist legislation to abolish the coloured franchise in South Africa,

Roy Campbell remarked to me, speaking of the Torch Commando, "In 1926 when we were in Natal there were just the three of us carrying hurricane lamps against the storm; now many people carry burning torches through the streets." And this too is the paradox of South Africa. As the forces of reaction have hardened, so the forces of emancipation have grown.

The collective conflicts and individual tensions, the mechanisms of self-deception, hypocrisy and abuse of power sketched so vividly in *Turbott Wolfe* are not peculiar to South Africa. They are a fundamental part of the human spirit and everywhere play the same sorry role in the turbulent story of our time. In America I found that colour prejudice in the south often assumes a more brutal, and in the north a more hypocritical, aspect than it does in South Africa, and with far less cause for fear. Nor are the coloured people themselves free of racialism. One of the most depressing experiences of my life has been witnessing, in places as far apart as Indonesia and Africa where I have taken part in the native struggle for emancipation, how to-day the abuses of power and the despotisms of the spirit that we thought we had abolished for ever are returning in a darker and more menacing form than ever before. In this sense, therefore, the implications of *Turbott Wolfe* are universal and immediate, and Mabel van der Horst remains the image of the love which is forever seeking to redeem the suffering inflicted by power on the powerless; in fact, to redeem power itself.

And here, perhaps, we are at the heart of the meaning of history. Since two thousand years back when the challenge of love in a world obsessed by power was first uttered in the Roman colony of Palestine, there has been implacable warfare in the human spirit and there can be no peace until it is

INTRODUCTION

resolved. History, it appears to me, even when it seems to be exclusively a matter of crude warfare over physical frontiers, ultimately is shown to have been a confused question of extending the marches of life into new, and inadequately understood, meaning. It is a record of an unending battle to make man obedient to his own greater awareness. History shows that, no matter how obstinate and adroit man's resistance, ultimately all are forced to obey this new meaning or to be submerged. In this sense South Africa seems to be an extreme example of an entire epoch denying its greater awareness. But what I have called "the growing forces of emancipation" in my country are those forces inspired by the conviction that South Africa, as has been proved by the world's past, cannot forever swim against the main stream of history. So I believe that, given time, like the rest of the world, my native country could still discover that she too must follow the inner march of history and allow the spirit of Mabel van der Horst to walk on and take her proper place in the centre of the stage. I could not believe this so firmly were it not for this book which, when all the signs were against it, came so mysteriously out of the mind of a lonely boy to bring about a deep sea-change in the imagination of my country.

I

I THINK Turbott Wolfe may have been a man of genius.
I hardly saw him from the time that I was at school with
him until he was about to die, at no great age, of a fever that
he had caught in Africa. He knew how ill he was, and sent
for me to come and see him at his lodgings at E——. I found
him in a ridiculous room, looking tired rather than ill as he
sat up in bed. His window gave on a slum that might have
been anywhere but near the sea, yet at night you could hear a
muffled noise of waves, while the day-time, always dingy
there, came with street noises, and sometimes in the afternoons seemed to become more dismal with the sounds of
football somewhere near at hand.

The room itself was so tawdry as to be grotesque. Patterns
of flowers, sewn or painted or printed in smudgy colours,
decorated the walls, the curtains, the linoleum on the floor,
the linen, the furniture; and they were all different. I felt obscured by all those scentless bouquets, but Turbott Wolfe
seemed so little obscured that he might have purposely designed those enormous bistre-and-green roses that were
tousled and garlanded up and down the coverlet on the bed;
and the wall behind his head, with its bouquets of brown
marguerites, its pomegranates and bows of ribbon and forget-
me-nots, became for him an ideal background.

He was dignified in a curious way perhaps peculiar to very
intelligent people. All the time that he was talking he seemed
profoundly excited, and now and then his gestures became,

like his narrative, erratic, but there was with him an assured grace, perhaps because of the fine culture that he had and because of the intense natural sensitiveness of his nature.

—There came to me a time—he said—not very long after I left school, when I found myself as lonely as it is possible to be. I was ill, and hardly recovered from the aftermath of adolescence. I came to feel as though circumstances had driven me with cunning deliberation and relentless activity to a point of complete isolation. I found myself with no friend, no passion, no anchor whatever.

My life seemed to be then a structure that had grown steadily without the least deviation from the architect's plan —every stone was being put in place, every malicious ornament. Lack of money; perhaps an extreme sensitiveness; a deep-rooted immovable cowardice; sudden flowers of courage—all these seemed due to an invisible constructor of my life, who must have been Gothic, so intent was he upon his work, so nice with satire.

But the cruel building was suddenly ruined. I was inflamed with the sun of a new day. Perhaps you remember——? I was suddenly ordered to Africa by some fool of a doctor.

My people sought, obtained, and paid nothing for advice that was considered good. I was to be started with a trading-station, in a region neither too civilized nor too remote. The prospect pleased me. I could think of nothing more thrilling than a small business, under my own eye, under my own hand, in which no halfpenny would be able to stray. A small business, I reflected, would be like an instrument. It would be entirely dependent on me for the music; for the volume, the pitch, the tone, the quality of the music. I thought then, as I think now, that trade is like art. Art is to the artist and trade is to the tradesman. I think the greatest illusion I know is that trade has anything to do with customers. It must have been so long ago, almost before history I should think, so very long ago quite plain that you must never, if you are to be a success in trade, in art, in politics, in life itself, you must *never* give people what they want. Give them what you want them to want. Then you are safe. But it is a platitude, and I digress.

You can imagine my delirious weeks of preparation. I rushed to and fro in the City buying what I was told to buy, because the people who sold me the stuff wanted to sell it to me.

"I like these," I would say to an elderly obstinate cunning respectable shirt-sleeved shop-walking citizen, with thirty years' uninterrupted experience of softs or roughs.

"O, no, sir," he would exclaim, in a whisper husky with astonishment, "not *those*! You would never sell *those* where you are going. But *these* now—you will have to have a few of *these*, even if you do not get them here. Everybody has *these*——"

"But I don't like them," I would say, for fun.

"Why! A standard line! You must have them! Go like hot cakes! Carry a nice little profit too! *These*——"

★ 2 ★

I also spent the little money I had of my own. I spent it freely buying books; paint; a piano; pens, ink and paper; a little furniture; and many odds and ends.

I was sorry to leave my people; I was devoted to them. But otherwise I sailed with no regrets, and with more excitement than hope.

I do not propose to bore you with a long account of the various difficulties I had at the start. A time came fairly soon when the shop began to run steadily with enough profit to give me a living. I had been fortunate enough to get the services of a remarkably steady 'civilized' native, by name Caleb Msomi, and it was due as much to him as to me that I was able to get the trading-station of Ovuzane established. It is the custom of the natives in those parts to do all their business in the morning, so my afternoons were nearly always free. I turned with immense enthusiasm to an immense number of different activities. I went from one to another, how restlessly you cannot imagine. You know that I once had ideas about a co-ordination of all the arts. I have always been pointed at as versatile. Is it a compliment? I have never been satisfied to plough only one furrow.

At Ovuzane I passed my time between trade and folk-lore and painting and writing and music, between sculpture and religion and handicrafts. I even got down to landscape-gardening. They have been pleased to tell me, one or two who have had the chance and I hope the wit to judge, that the work I did during that period had value. They have been kind; I have been flattered. After a time I was surprised to get a communication (I couldn't call it a letter) from a very distinguished acquaintance whose wish it was to visit me at Ovuzane for the purpose of undertaking to compile a carefully illustrated record of what I had done. The man was Tyler-Harries. He had quite a name in those days, but you wouldn't hear much about him now, I suppose. I was half afraid and half contemptuous of him; he was a silly *poseur*, but he had a wonderful grasp of things, and a sort of way with him.

Eventually I found myself at Dunnsport to meet the man. Tyler-Harries, man of means, emerged on long and pointed feet from the *Rochester Castle*, polished and distant and distrustful, a maker of editions-de-luxe, founder of the Pomegranate Press and of the Pomegranate Press Society, publishers who, as the *London Review* declared, "have given us so many rare and beautiful and surprising works"; given us, that paper omitted to state, given us, as a matter of fact, at ten or twelve guineas a time. Perhaps I have a mercenary mind: that is not my idea of being given a book.

The only thing, I said to myself, as Tyler-Harries strutted down the gangway of the *Rochester Castle*, that could have brought him to Africa was the chance of making an edition even more rare and beautiful and surprising than the things that were said about him in London.

We stayed at the Mountjoy Hotel, where you may see all sorts of people at any time.

"My *dear* man," exclaimed Tyler-Harries in his loudest and wickedest manner, "how many fish there are here out of water!"

At Ovuzane we argued a great deal, but Tyler-Harries worked fourteen hours a day at his notes, and his drawings, and his photographs, and his very large correspondence. I think his book would have been better than my work that it described. I say 'would have been' because the great man chose to return in a rotten cargo-boat round the East Coast instead of in a first-class liner by the West. The thing got wrecked. But mark this, the fool was not content to part with his manuscripts; he must needs go and get himself drowned too. I was told that Tyler-Harries had last been seen with a coloured stewardess. They were both very far gone in raw cane-spirit, kindly supplied by the lady.

I spent a couple of days in Dunnsport after seeing off Tyler-Harries, and in the evenings I amused myself by attending at a kind of fairground in the slums, to have a look at 'Schönstein's Better Shows'. I knew Schönstein, you see. He was on the boat when I first went out. A prodigious Jew, he was, with egg-yellow eye-brows. Rich. He directed his precious shows (they travel all over Africa) from Johannesburg. His wife, I remember, was a little plump partridge with nerves of brass. She was barefaced by day and barebacked by night.

I went that time to 'Schönstein's Better Shows' at Dunnsport to enjoy, as I thought, the hurdy-gurdy music and the coloured lights and noises. I was a little startled to find an extraordinary mixture of races at the fair, which was managed by one Judy Frenkel, a young man with jewellery and fat. He had a chestnut-coloured suit and patent-leather boots with cloth tops, and he lost no time in informing me that he wore no underclothing but his socks and a silk shirt. I had introduced myself to him as a friend of Mr Schönstein.

* 3 *

Round us as we talked circulated a crowd of black, white and coloured people: English, Dutch, Portuguese, nondescript were the whites; Bantu, Lembu, Christianized and aboriginal, Mohammedan negroes were the blacks; and the coloured were all colours and all races fused. It came upon me suddenly in that harsh polyglot gaiety that I was living in Africa; that there is a question of colour. Where's my diary?

Here it is. I cannot do better than read to you what I wrote at the time.

Schönstein's Better Shows

It is the steam-organ's function to bewitch the merry-go-round with noise: wailing and palpitating, to drive the prancing figures faster and faster; to produce a final din, brandishing a tune like an insult; and then of a sudden to leave the scene silent and deserted.

The merry-go-round, brightly lit and brightly coloured, is garishly desolate, while the empty voice of the dago who summons people to ride upon it is as its own voice, articulate, pleading for a tawdry misery to be soothed. The clamour is dead that drugged the brain and excited the nerves, so one man throws away a cigarette, and another turns with a shrug. Another talks in confidence with one of the dollish women who sell tickets for side-shows, sitting here and there, each in a kiosk like a monstrous hood, dark without and light within.

Above them the great wheel towers and clatters with coloured lights, its passengers two by two in little cars soaring pathetically into the night, lapsing swiftly to earth, people obsessed with an illusion; now as they appear leaning out to watch a dispute at one of the games of chance, where a cheapjack with custard-yellow hair and a false buttonhole is at blows with an Indian youth because of sixpence. After a moment the game proceeds, electric light upthrown on vivid faces—white, yellow, black—set like masks, or moving like the faces of marionettes.

Esoteric movements stir the crowd, at one place ribald, watching a gross European in one of the swing-boats with a girl sitting facing him, her back to those watching. The man propels the boat to a great height, laughing whitely under a small black moustache at the girl's evident fear; but the swing is soon finished, and she stands up, the man descending to help her out. Even when she is on the ground he holds fast her hand, and suddenly stoops to kiss her. Quickly she turns her head—the idle crowd breaks out with lascivious comment, seeing her to be not white—and the kiss falls on her neck.

She is enraged. She flings away from him, momentarily defiant under an arc-lamp. Plainly to be seen are the faint pallor of her ashen-yellow skin and the tip of her mulberry-pink derisive tongue.

Bawdy laughter. A sally in the darkness. A pursuit by the crowd. And after a time the man saunters back to his friends, fluttering one hand high above his head in lewd farewell.

Is it a flag on a ruin, that hand? a portent, preceding a half-caste world?

—That—said Turbott Wolfe—is what I wrote in my diary. I began to concern myself with the colour of people's skins. Travelling home to Ovuzane I found myself looking at the natives with new eyes. I suspected myself of taking sides with them. An incident happened that seemed oddly to confirm my suspicion. It was on the platform at Aucampstroom, the station for Ovuzane. The only one of my white neighbours, except the missionary, that I knew by sight seemed to approach me. In an attempt to act the hearty Colonial I held out my hand to him. Quite frankly. He sneered at it and turned away.

It was a shock. It was intensified by the obscurity of the man's behaviour. I groped for a reason, and could find none. So I departed, on the Sunday following my return home, for the Hlanzeni Mission Station, to get the advice of the missionary, Karl Nordalsgaard, the only white man of quality I had so far come across in Lembuland. Hlanzeni is only a few miles from Ovuzane, and it was not my first visit.

The very remarkable old man ushered me gracefully into a dark airless comfortable musty room, thronged with dusty books and dirty furniture. We drank coffee, and afterwards he produced a couple of long-stemmed meerschaum pipes.

"These," he said, "belong to my student days." There were many wrinkles on his forehead.

He gave me one of the pipes and tobacco to smoke, and I told him of what had happened at Aucampstroom station.

"I know," was all he said, nodding his old heavy head.

I did not see till then that his fat elderly good-hearted housekeeper was standing framed in a doorway in the shadows beyond him. Her name was Rosa Grundso. The natives loved her for her good heart. She was as sound as a bell.

"Ach, don't you worry, Mr Wolfe," she said now in a quiet imperturbable voice. "It is only jealousy. They know you are better than they are. That is all. It is the same with Mr Nordalsgaard. They know he is better than they are, too. Ach, it is only jealousy. It is no good to worry."

"You see," she added, "they know you have culture. They know they haven't. That is enough for them."

"I suppose," I said, "that they would not approve of my having a studio, and taking an interest in anything beyond other people's business."

"I know," said Nordalsgaard, wagging his profoundly melancholy old head. He was in complete sympathy with me. There is no sympathy that has the peculiar tenderness of an old man's sympathy. I was utterly soothed.

And yet for a long time Nordalsgaard seemed to me utterly unfathomable: it took a long time for me to establish for myself facts about his past, his character, his predecessor. And even then much remained obscure. I could see from the beginning that he had an immense influence over the natives, but it was an influence that worked on a hidden plane. There was nothing obvious about it. There was no 'muscular Christianity'. Rather was Nordalsgaard like an immense electric storage battery, full of nervous energy, in secret communication, in secret touch with each individual native soul (I am not talking about moral influence: I said *immense* influence) and producing here or there, suddenly or slowly, probably unexpectedly, a reaction that would have all the appearance of being spontaneous. The electric wires were there, but the switch, if you see what I mean, was only turned on by circumstances.

Nordalsgaard was a Norwegian, a survival of an ancient type of missionary, a Lutheran-Catholic, unmercenary, a scholar, a gentleman, looking to his work to reward him only with the affection of the half-awakening consciousness of the simian, mystical, child-like, man-like and woman-like obscure attractive soul of the African.

He was a man whose nature it was to break a mountain of rock if only he might find a little vein of gold. For nearly forty years he had been at Hlanzeni, successor to the almost legendary Bishop Klodquist, a prodigious patriarch, a neo-Viking, an incredible pioneer, a hirsute autocrat.

Klodquist, with mid-Victorian obstinacy, had brought himself to the aboriginals with a reticule of black leather, containing a Bible and a bottle of *vin ordinaire*. He had no pyjamas, and not a word of Lembu.

Three times his church was burnt down (once by accident and twice in malice) and three times he rebuilt it, lastly in solid stone, as it still stands. But now it is insured against both

66

fire and civil commotion. Klodquist's worst friends (no one could be said to be his enemy) were the lions. He dug trenches round his mission and filled them with fire. He attacked the lions with knives, this tragic Tartarin, he assailed them with shot from a monstrous blunderbuss. And if in his day there had been a little more perfection in cameras, no doubt he would have gone against the lions with a camera too. He might even have been tempted to make moving pictures as modern big-game hunters have done—*moving* pictures only in that they are not stationary.

A battered magic-lantern was good enough for Klodquist. On great occasions he would present the Life of Christ in thirty scenes, made in Germany. To you and to me the slides would have appeared to be permutations and combinations in the grouping of a number of gaunt German Jews with small eyes and gaunt German Jewesses with large eyes, draped in yards and yards and yards of natty shirting in the newest stripes, or in assorted lengths of tomato-red plush, grass-green or bilge-brown.

Klodquist thought they were beautiful, and the heathen itched to embrace Christianity as soon as they saw them.

Age following rapidly upon a seemingly interminable middle-age decided Klodquist to marry; so he travelled laboriously, in an age when travelling was laborious, to Norway, and returned almost immediately with a lovely young cousin as his bride. She, poor creature, was so bored with Hlanzeni that she fell to painting a portrait of her Klodquist for the church, double life-size, in full canonicals; which being completed she died of fever.

Klodquist survived her by a number of years, and when he eventually died, in the same way that a vast ship sinking draws towards it the tiny craft of the shipwrecked and a multitude of those struggling in the water, so Klodquist sinking into his grave drew half the natives of Lembuland. They were camped out in thousands at Hlanzeni, and when all was over can only have been succeeded by an unnatural calm.

This was the tradition which Nordalsgaard inexplicably came to maintain. I say 'inexplicably', because at twenty-one he had had birth, brains, breeding, education and money. He was also young and good-looking. The reason for his coming must have been something to do with a woman: he used to mumble vaguely about 'my student days', toying in his hand with a meerschaum pipe, festooned with red braid and tassels.

I do not suppose that Nordalsgaard ever was so great as Klodquist. Like the bishop he was an autocrat, but unlike the bishop he was not a dictator. Nordalsgaard cut a figure, but after Klodquist not a fabulous one. He was loved, but not worshipped. Where his predecessor had been a god, Nordalsgaard was a demigod. Nevertheless, I tell you, I repeat it —Nordalsgaard had an immense influence with the natives. And because of his quality, I was able to leave him that day curiously fortified in spirit. I had seen him in his own setting, wrinkled and care-worn with the fatigues of missionary statesmanship, a career that is more gruelling (even to the insensitive) than political statesmanship, because it cannot save itself from dealing in hearts instead of in blood: wrinkled and careworn, but calm, and associated with the admirable Miss Rosa Grundso. And because they were fortified, I was fortified. I was fortified against struggles that I knew would come. There would be conflict between myself and the white; there would be conflict between myself and the black. There would be the unavoidable question of colour. It is a question to which every man in Africa, black, white or yellow, must provide his own answer.

* 4 *

One afternoon at Ovuzane I had been intensely occupied, with four natives, in working out some Lembu folk-tunes. We had been at it, I suppose, three or four hours without a break. The natives had played till their fingers were nearly numb. They were sitting on the floor at one end of the vast room, as large as a church, that I used as a workroom and studio. They were shining with sweat. In that room it was dusk. We were labouring at the final version of a theme.

What do you think? A stinking motor-car drew up at the very door. I had to go out into the dazzling sunlight. There was an ugly fellow with a female. Neither of them seemed to have any manners or any brains. I had to ask him his name. It was Bloodfield. I managed to get from him the information that he was a farmer at Ovuzanyana. The girl was his sister-in-law. They had come to see me.

"It is very noble of you to come so far, over such a rough road," I said. "You ought to have brought Mrs Bloodfield with you."

The man sniffed: the girl sniggered. They were not only ill-mannered: they were gauche. I felt inclined to tell them what I thought of them, but I said instead:

"You'd better come into the studio and have some tea."

The girl did not seem to be in any way affected by what I said, but I noticed that she had an extremely fine complexion with her too fair hair.

As for the man, his face took on the sort of expression that you might look for on a charwoman's if you asked her to enter a night-club. Bloodfield was a lean ungainly man with

69

a hen's head, with small bright black mean eyes in his thin red face.

We went in, and I turned aside to order tea. But Blood-field's face was set in malicious violence: his pig's hair seemed almost to bristle. He was looking at the natives, who were sitting quiet and beautiful in the quiet gloom under the high windows.

"Surely you don't have these blooming niggers in here?" he shouted.

"You see that I do."

"But what on earth are they doing?"

"We have given the afternoon to music," I said.

He grunted, looking at me as if I was a dangerous lunatic. My eyes sought the pleasing carnation of his sister-in-law's cheeks, and she began to ask a great number of silly questions.

I suppose there would not be anything very remarkable about such a girl here, for instance, at E——; but she seemed at Ovuzane a being from another world. I had a sudden whim that I should like to paint her, and I asked her to come over and sit for me, not in the least supposing that she would.

"I should love to," she said simply.

"I don't think you'll be able to get away," said Bloodfield, looking hard at her.

"I'll manage," she said. It was the first sign of character I had seen in her. By the way, what is character? Character is the determination to get one's own way.

Well, she came. I had planned that she should sit under a tree in my garden, an indigenous tree with ice-green leaves; with a native girl that I was often drawing at that time she should sit, their arms interlaced. The picture, for rather an elaborate reason, was to be called *Souvenir of Dostoievsky*. But the extraordinary thing is that nothing would induce the girl to sit with the native. Colour prejudice, I suppose. She said she would be only too pleased to sit by herself.

"Good Lord," I said, "what's wrong? I suppose the native girl is human?" I said I must have her with the other, or not at all. I may have been a little brusque.

She rushed away; and for a long five minutes I heard the car she was driving climbing away up the hills. But I couldn't see it.

The native girl came to me pathetically and sat down at my feet. I thought for a moment that she might compensate me—but I suddenly felt as cold towards her as if she had been a monkey. I got up and walked away.

Bloodfield never spoke to me again all the years I was in Lembuland, and he made a practice of turning his back to me whenever we met in public. The story about the model was nastily mangled, and found its way back to me in varying versions for years. It even got into an offensive little newspaper that they print in Aucampstroom, cautiously and vulgarly worded.

I began to learn the hard lesson that in Lembuland it is considered a crime to regard the native as anything even so high as a mad wild animal. I was so surprised that I began to seek with keenness for information about the relations between blacks and whites in those parts. I set myself to find out all that I could about the blacks and whites themselves, about their points of view; and about missions and missionaries. I began to ask everybody questions without number, travelling farther afield.

Caleb Msomi, the storeman, was a trustworthy and amusing encyclopædia of local matters. He enlightened me very soon about a man called Flesher, one of my nearest and nastiest neighbours. There was a story that a native girl had once spat in his eye, quite spontaneously, out of sheer disdain.

I went to look at Flesher. I may be a coward myself, but I have never seen a man with smaller courage and less manliness about him. Everything to do with him was mean and puny and contemptible. He wore a beard and strutted like a mountebank (but without a mountebank's style) in breeches and leggings, carrying his five feet of wretchedness as though he wished you to believe that the responsibilities of a continent were transported about on those two thin legs.

He used to live on such maize-meal as might be left over by his servants, helping himself out of their pot, though he never had a good word to say for them. It was his dearest pleasure to find himself among strangers, and to be able to announce to them:

"I never drink tea. I never buy meat. I never touch bread. Mealie-meal is good enough for me."

On one occasion when he said this I heard a man make an enemy of Flesher for life by the comment:

"Well, I've often heard of men living like niggers, but you're the first I ever heard boast of it."

Flesher was too poor a thing to be any man's friend, so he was certainly not worth having as an enemy. All the same, he used to do more harm by gossip and mischief-making and petty scandalmongering than any woman I ever heard of. It was his most cherished plan to frequent the houses of newcomers; to accept their unlimited hospitality; and, if they were so indiscreet, their confidence. He would then run like a hunted thing from house to house (they were very many miles apart) with his own version of the family's most personal concerns. After he had glutted himself with lies he would ignore his former hosts entirely, and return home to his mealie-meal like a dog to his vomit again.

One woman who came to live in those parts had been fore-warned. She was so disgusted with Flesher's appearance (his blood must have been in a rotten state, for his face and hands were covered with scorbutic sores) that she cunningly asked him to stay away because he frightened the children.

Living alone, I could not help dwelling on these people in my thoughts far more than they were worth. Give me a good old criminal lunatic any day, rather than ask me to breathe the same air as Flesher and Bloodfield: I should feel so much more at ease. And seeing continually incessant lines of natives trooping in and out of the store I turned my feelings, in escape from the unclean idea of Flesher and Bloodfield, far too much into sympathy with the aboriginal. I found myself charmed with unending euphonious conversations in Lembu, simple and intimate. My eye was training itself to admire to excess the over-developed marvellous animal grace of each Lembu individual. I was becoming ecstatic over the bright-eyed ingenuousness of every child; over the patriarchal grace of each old man, over the youthful grace of every young one; over the aged women, large-eyed tender women who were mothers, warm-handed tender daughters who were lovers. I was losing my balance. I remembered that every civilized white man, who considers himself sensitive, in touch with native peoples in his daily life should hold in his heart an image of the failure of Gauguin. Was it a failure? I asked myself: and in the question itself thought I suspected danger. I found myself all at once overwhelmed with a suffocating sensation of universal black darkness. Blackness. I was being sacrificed, a white lamb, to black Africa.

It may have been a disorder of the nerves; it may have

been prevision. In consequence I went oftener away to Au-campstroom.

That town lies on a bleak plateau, colder and higher by far than my own low-lying home at Ovuzane. Aucampstroom was an outpost of the voortrekking Dutch: they could pene-trate no farther to the north and north-east, being in too close proximity to the borders of Swedish East Africa, foreign ter-ritory; and no farther to the east and south-east in the direc-tion of Ovuzane and the greater part of Lembuland, because that was native territory under special protection. It was from the west and the south that the Dutch had come, a few families venturing farther than any. Venturing like Scythians over rocky illimitable wastes, in those days unmeasured, they had come in mighty tented waggons that creaked and groaned, crude magnificent arks, on stupendous wheels, forced up and down the roadless uneven hills by straining teams of titanic oxen.

There were large gross men with flag-like beards, peasant-minds, and patriarchal names and manners; begetters of chil-dren. There were large gross women with wooden limbs and loud voices, bearers of children, their harsh heads hidden in prodigious flapping sun-bonnets of sheer black, as wickedly significant as the fell wings of unknown birds of ill-omen, in a landscape of clear dusty blue, and in an atmosphere as subtle as time and as vast as eternity.

Children came with them of all ages, babies and brats, quiet and mostly fascinated and bright-eyed (with black bright eyes like darting beetles, as all children have) and emulative (as all children are) of parents so wonderful as to be almost incredible. And young women with love insatiable, proud in their young womanliness; and young men were there, active, with young unshaven beards like bright wire in the sun.

Under the hoods of the waggons were secreted household goods—under every single hood a big black bible, the holiest possession of each single family, massive, four-square, full of bitter biblical wisdom: and its pages turned oftenest by patriarchal thumbs in times of stress. "Adversity", as is written in each of those bibles, "teacheth a man to pray; prosperity never."

Aucampstroom owes its existence to these *voortrekkers*, and especially to their leader, Petrus Aucamp, to whom, as to his followers, guns served for grace, powder for polish, and meat for manners. While Metternich was dying the broad ambitious roads of Aucampstroom were being laid out, intersecting each other to form spacious *erven* for the homes of the elders; and all the outlying mountains, rough with rocks and smooth with grass, were being apportioned into farms as large as counties. But when I came to Aucampstroom—said Turbott Wolfe—I could not persuade myself that the hopes of its founders had matured. After all the intervening years it was only a *dorp* with a few thousand inhabitants. The farms had been divided equally, according to the wills of the patriarchs, among their sons and daughters, and re-divided among the children of the third and fourth generations until many of them could no longer scratch a living out of the sour soil, and had migrated to the large distant towns, where they had degenerated, lacking balance, into poor whites. The population of the town itself was now half composed of the descendants of English colonists, and there were also Jews, Greeks, Indians, a great number of 'coloured people', and a location full of Lembus. There was a magistracy; a Dutch Reformed church, a pretentious building; an English church like a shed; a Wesleyan chapel, much bigger; a railway station; and a great deal of backbiting.

I had been provided originally with a letter of introduction to the English church priest, who was adorned with the style of the Reverend Justinian Fotheringhay, and it was before his door that I most often found myself when I went to Aucampstroom to take my thoughts off Ovuzane. In the middle of that front door there appeared to be an electric bell, but it was unlike any other bell upon any other front door I have ever seen. Instead of that tingling far away that an expectant ear may catch from the labyrinths of a mansion; instead of that silence (even more impressive) when you know the bell is ringing, but the ringing is out of earshot; instead of the almost plastic silence of a bell that is broken; the front door bell of the Fotheringhays gave forth upon the slightest touch a loud alarming clangour from within the very panels of the door itself. I suppose everybody that touched for the first time that ebony button, even with the delicacy of a butterfly, must have started back a pace for fear. But the second time, after the bell, you would hear, listening intently, the rumour of a muttered conference; and the door would open, disclosing to you the considerable parson or his tiny wife. In either case (if you did not know already the two Fotheringhays; or if you had not heard of Turgenev's Fomishka and Fimishka; or if you were not familiar with the type of old gentlemanly priest, like Nordalsgaard and Fotheringhay, stranded on the rock of his own consciousness in that bewildering sea that is life in modern Africa) in either case a shock awaited you. Whatever size you might be yourself you were almost bound to be startled by the apparition of a colossus in black with a rosy face like a relief-map, or by his wife, who was to her husband as the partridge to the dodo. They never came together to the door. One was hurriedly delegated by their parliament of two, and the other hovered assiduously in a room upon the left, awaiting your arrival.

The room upon the left told you at once that the house was built in the Afrikander tradition. The Dutch love to place a large living-room, like a Roman *atrium*, in the middle of their dwellings, with rooms all round it. You would know what I mean if you had ever sat in Dutch houses and raised your voice to try and drown the too personal noises in the daughters' bedroom a few yards from your elbow!

This, the Fotheringhays' living-room, had at one end a large window looking upon the *stoep*, and at the other french-windows opening upon the back-*stoep* and the garden. One of the side walls had a door into the hall and another into the kitchen, each protected with a large folding screen covered with scarlet baize. Between the doors was a fireplace which I never saw without a fire. Winter and summer, whenever I entered the room, the grate was banked up with red-hot coals; smoke was rushing up the chimney; the fender was choked with ashes; and a large coarse white cat called Timothy was sitting with its eyes fixed on the fire and its mind groping for pleasure in the confused recollections of instinct.

The wall on the opposite side of the room was practically hidden by an upright piano and a monumental sideboard covered with books and cruets, nevertheless it was broken by three doors leading into three rooms, of which only one, the farthest from the hall door, was never referred to by name. It was the bedroom of the old couple. The other two were known as The Spare Room and Mr Fotheringhay's Dressing Room. They were spoken of with such an air of importance, with such an awe-struck whisper, that they might well have been ballrooms or banqueting-halls. For a long time I was unable to see the inside of these two rooms, but I was bitten with a curiosity that was nearly malicious. However, I came unexpectedly to lunch at the Rectory one cold day before the old man had returned from a call, and upon asking to be allowed to wash my hands I was ushered with ceremony into that holy of holies, Mr Fotheringhay's Dressing Room. His wife, with a polite skirmish, indicated a wash-stand, and disappeared.

It was less like a dressing-room than anything I have ever seen. It was a bear-garden. The whole place was littered with rubbish—mirrors, old straps and bottles and pipes and feathers and tins and papers; mouse-traps; toothless combs, brushes without bristles, chairs without backs, tables without legs. In the midst of this confusion was the wash-stand, very small and grimy, with a lurch when you touched it, like a man too drunk to be obstinate. It supported as well as it could a little tin basin full of dirty soapy water, and a half-used cake of soap grey with dust, and a towel that must have served the Devil, if he had ever had occasion to visit himself upon this inaccessible sanctum, for a door-mat.

There was no view from the window of the Rev. Justinian Fotheringhay's Dressing Room, because it was like an eye that is bleary. It seemed to have been deliberately tarred and feathered. The room was eerie with a greyish light, made stranger by the sifting layers, the drifts, the plumes and bouquets of dust that blurred every projection and filled every hollow. It seemed to me that the room was haunted. Something had died there, choked with dust—perhaps an idea.

When I had entered the room Mrs Fotheringhay had said: "I'm afraid we're rather untidy."

"Not at all," I had made answer, with a bow.

When I had pretended to wash I was not sorry to escape.

As I stepped back into the living-room I caught a glimpse, through the large lace-curtained window at the end of the room, of the cold stone tower of the new Dutch Reformed church set above bleak angular iron roofs in a bitter sky; and of an eddy of wind in the street lifted in a cloud of sulphur-coloured dust, twirling round and round till it vanished.

It was a view upon which Mrs Fotheringhay's small pale eyes must often have been fixed. Indeed, I caught her occasionally in conversation (for I sat generally with my back to the window) looking over my shoulder at the dismal stony newness of that cold and foreign tower, as though she expected that that small hope that lived in her head, like a flea on an elephant, would be answered with a sudden marvel, a miraculous appearance of a fiery radiant archangel alighting on the tower, a young man, with white wings like a swan and a warm manner, to transport her at once and for ever from the house she never left to some smooth and happy other life—even, perhaps, to that castle, to live in which she had more than once declared it to be the summit of her ambition.

"I should like," she used to say with great emphasis, "what I should really like would be to live in a castle. A beautiful castle. By the sea. In Scotland."

Once in a portfolio of drawings and paintings in water-colour she found, as we turned over her girlish hieroglyphics, a highly-coloured mediæval fortress on a rocky island.

"Ah," she exclaimed in triumph, "that's Drumdoodle Castle! You must have heard of it? My father took it for the summer once when I was sixteen. It *was* beautiful."

"Now," she said, pointing to a dark small daub, "do you know who that is? That's Mr Fotheringhay! Standing on the ramparts. O, and I had such a lovely horse. His name was

Beau. He *was* beautiful. My father gave ninety guineas for him. But we lost him. He was stolen. We never got him back. It *was* sad."

Of conversation at the Rectory there seemed to be only one possible form—a monologue from either the parson or his wife, punctuated with flat contradictions from the listening partner, and varied with the most charming disputes in miniature. It was like a river of words that kept on coming to a fresh turn; that was thwarted a moment; and then flowed away in another direction as majestically as ever.

The monologue was ejected with the spontaneity of a song-bird's between the two rows of small cheap wax-white false teeth that were ever at war like opposing cohorts in the tiny damp pink cave that served as a mouth the Rev. Justinian Fotheringhay. If the monologue came from him it must needs be nothing but reminiscence and family folk-lore. If his wife wasn't there, the dear old man would lean forward in his chair by the fire with a fine hand on each thigh, and a cumbrous pendulous paunch like Falstaff's hanging down before him like a bag of jelly. With a screen of scarlet baize as a background he would wag his large broad head and tell you in measured terms of his very great and continual anxiety about the state of his wife's health.

"The doctor says I am ill," he assured me, "but Mrs Fotheringhay is much worse. She will not take care of herself. She slipped down on her back about a year ago and hurt herself very badly. She hasn't been out of the house for nine months. And then last March down she went again on a beastly slippery floor——"

"No, I didn't," declared Mrs Fotheringhay, suddenly appearing in a doorway, with a pile of house-linen balanced on her arm.

"But, my dear, you did," her husband asserted.

"No, it was in April."

"O, very well then, it was in April."

My chief pleasure at the Rectory was got when Mrs Fotheringhay herself settled down to talk, and it was a frequent pleasure, because she took every opportunity of rebuilding, as accurately as a castle in Spain, the varieties of her past, including her father's castle in Scotland. She was a very small woman, with the dignity of a duchess and the vivacity of a child. She used to wear a long thick black dress like a monk's habit, with a high collar and long tight sleeves. It was tight about the bust and down to the hips, with a copious skirt, and unadorned except for a row of round cloth buttons as large as grapes from throat to foot. It was always the same garment, and yet the souvenirs of soup and porridge and candle-grease and flour all down the front never seemed to get more or less. Mrs Fotheringhay wore no jewellery but her wedding-ring. Her hair was dragged back in a few short strands and knotted up in a bun. She would talk for ever of what had long since happened; but occasionally she found another topic in native servants.

"O, we do have such bother with the servants. They are such curious creatures. You wouldn't believe it, but we have to do everything ourselves."

After this I couldn't help noticing the servants each time I went to the Rectory. There was one I remember especially, a tall fierce-looking woman of a lightish-brown colour. In hot weather she used to wear a huge open-work straw hat that flapped on her shoulders; and on bleaker days a brown woollen cap, fitting her head closely. She used to wait at table in better clothes than Mrs Fotheringhay had seen for many years, and I was fascinated to find on her face as she snaffled the dishes off the table a smile acuter than Voltaire's, the expression of a fixed and mordant cynicism. I followed her movements carefully for some time, and came to note that as soon as she left the table her sneer faded, coming back as soon only as she herself came back. It was the fatuous face of one without a heart, whose place it is to serve lunatics; the face of an empress washing the feet of beggars; the confident delightful mien of the forewarned victim of a practical joke.

Mrs Fotheringhay caught me stalking with my eyes her maidservant, and she leant forward with an air of surprising benevolence.

"She's a teacher in the native school in the location," she whispered. "A little difficult, you know. They want to *take* so many things. She always swears she doesn't. I found her little boy (a nice little black boy in a jersey) outside the kitchen door one day with a wheelbarrow. I said, 'Alice, why has he brought a wheelbarrow?' What do you think? She was going to load it up with knives and forks——"

"Evidently a business woman," her husband commented, quaking with mirth.

"I don't think it's funny," said the old woman, with round eyes.

But the predatory Alice seemed to stay on, and her table-sneer stayed on too.

Once I arrived to lunch at the Rectory when there was no servant at all. It was an elaborate meal, and an unexpected profusion of silver and glass seemed to me then to give every excuse for the lustful eyes of the long brown Alice.

I was penned in as usual with chairs and screens, my back roasted at the fire, and I was powerless to get to the aid of Mrs Fotheringhay, who shuffled backwards and forwards with quantities of food she had cooked herself. I can see her now, setting four or five puddings down at once, and then reviewing the table with a lift of her what-next eyebrows to note what she had forgotten.

"Do you like apples?" she inquired, waving vaguely an enormous silver spoon. "We used to have such beautiful apples at home. My father got them from abroad. They *were* beautiful."

"No, he didn't," said the rector.

"But, my dear, they did come from abroad."

"They didn't. They came from Yorkshire."

"Did they? Very well, then." She turned to me. "My father got them from Yorkshire."

We began talking about Yorkshire, and about the old Yorkshire family of d'Elvadere.

"I wonder if you know that there is a d'Elvadere in this district," said Mr Fotheringhay. "He works for a widow, a Mrs Dunford. Dissenters. Her husband was very much disliked. This is a very interesting old man, they tell me. I don't think I know him by sight. But of course with that name he ought to be a gentleman. O yes, I remember now, his father once held the living of F——. Before my time, of course. The d'Elvaderes are a mad family. This poor chap drank, they tell me. But he must be a very interesting old man. You ought to try and meet him. The d'Elvaderes were connected somehow with the Dukes of Floodwater. The twelfth Lord Fotheringhay, my great-grandfather, married one of the last Duke's daughters. He was rather an amusing man. I mean my great-grandfather. He was very dirty and untidy—didn't care how he looked.

"A woman caught sight of his nails once at an important dinner-party. 'O, Lord Fotheringhay,' she couldn't help exclaiming, 'how filthy your hands are!' He turned to her very solemnly. He was a little pompous. 'Madam,' he answered, 'that's nothing. *You should see my feet!*' "

I tried more than once unsuccessfully to open Fotheringhay's lips on the subject of Flesher and Bloodfield, but he would only damn the type generally, vaguely and guardedly. I could not get him to be personal. On the subject of missionaries his silence was virulent. He knew them for what they are.

I felt it was my duty to return some of the hospitality of the rector and his wife, but Mrs Fotheringhay would not leave the house, and her husband would not leave Mrs Fotheringhay, so the little reunions at the Rectory got farther and farther apart: I did not like to trespass too far on their kindness. And an incident happened that drove me thankfully to stay more contentedly at home at Ovuzane, watching and admiring the natives.

What happened was this. One evening I was just leaving the Fotheringhays. I stepped off the *stoep* almost into the arms of a woman called Cossie van Honk, nicknamed locally Aucampstroom's Wife. Her nickname was a guide to her profession. She was the wife of the whole dorp. She wasn't an ordinary prostitute. She was as much a public institution as the Town Hall. In the warm dusk I saw that her wrinkled face was ghastly with cheap powder, heavy with paint, pouting vilely. A hideous mask. She stank of scent, and in the quiet dark street I heard as I stood the patter of her feet and the rustling of her silks, as she went deliberately and purposefully about her business, with a cachou on her tongue.

The greatest obscenity was that in the daytime she was a certificated midwife.

It was a very strong emotion, this spasm of disgust at close physical proximity to the creature. I may not be fastidious, but I hope I am clean.

I tell you honestly, I was glad to get back to Ovuzane. I had not been giving the shop the attention it deserved just lately. I don't want you to think that I had ever been really out of sympathy with the natives: it was simply that their existence, their *blackness*, if you see what I mean, had seemed too much for me.

Before I thoroughly settled down again I made a journey by car to Ovuzanyana, up in the mountains, to the farm that belonged to the dissenting widow, Mrs Dunford, for the sole purpose of meeting the man d'Elvadere. He did not live, it appeared, at the farm-house, but in his own *rondavels* at an outpost two or three miles away. Mrs Dunford directed me. She was a talkative old woman with a great opinion of herself, and never anything of importance to say. I confess that I was more interested in her housekeeper, a young Dutch-woman, introduced as Miss van der Horst. She brought me a cup of tea in a sort of offhand way. Mrs Dunford called her Mabel. 'Mabel van der Horst', I repeated to myself: I was rather taken with her.

★ 5 ★

The manners of Francis d'Elvadere (I noticed that every-body spoke of him as Old Frank) had something about them as ducal as his ancestry. He was an enormous man, with weep-ing moustaches of a shining reddish copper colour standing magnificently off his rosy face.

I found him standing outside one of his *rondavels* mending a plough. I explained who I was, and why I had come, and in a minute we seemed to be the oldest friends. He was soon telling me how he gave up drinking, and then he walked me round to the back to show me a mountain of empty beer-bottles, of green glass, winking in the sun.

"Those aren't mine," he said. "They were left there by my predecessor: but I might have got down to that, too."

It was a prodigious sight, this monument of a man who had drunk himself to death.

D'Elvadere I found to be thoroughly the pioneer, but a voluptuous pioneer, a very different type from the *voortrekker*. In the far-off days of gold-rushes he had rushed to the gold with everybody else, days when one bathed, water being scarce, in gallons of champagne. He told of Goldenville, that vast city, when it was a mining camp. He had known Golden Liz, the first woman up there, who ought to have her place beside the great women of history. Her beauty conducted her through an astounding career. At first she used to put herself up for auction, parading nude upon the first billiard-table in Goldenville with a brilliant smile, before a roomful of admiring miners. Afterwards she had been the mistress, and almost the wife, of the great Nigel Blades, empire-builder, the founder of our fortunes in Bladesia. Poor Golden Liz, when her beauty faded, she entered a nunnery.

While I was talking to d'Elvadere a young native came up to him on a bicycle. He had brought him a note. D'Elvadere shook hands with him quite frankly, as man to man. Ha, I thought, what would Flesher and Bloodfield say to that, who have never known a generous feeling or done a generous action in all their puny lives? The native was introduced to me as Zachary Msomi. "He is going to be a parson," d'Elvadere explained.

I remembered that I had seen him sometimes in the store at Ovuzane. His surname was the same as Caleb's, my storeman. I remembered that they were cousins. I shook hands with him too, and somehow it gave me a curious thrill to give an external sign of the difference between my point of view and that of people like Flesher and Bloodfield; to thwart them, as it were, in public. "Shake hands with a native!" they would have shrieked. "Why, they are just like animals!" If they are like animals, I reflected, in that is their chief charm.

I left d'Elvadere feeling soothed. I had detected under his mild bearing a surging intolerance that I admire. I had felt, as they say, 'at home with him'.

Within a week I had nearly made a fool of myself. One morning Caleb told me a nickname that the natives had given me. A Lembu word meaning Chastity. 'Chastity Wolfe,' I said vainly, looking at myself in the glass. My mother used to say:

"Men are such fools."

You will agree, when I tell you that I was very strongly attracted, that very afternoon, by a native girl. This was something I hadn't bargained for. I had been looking all this time at the natives with a quizzing eye. Now I had only myself to blame.

The girl came into the store and took my breath away. She took away the breath of Chastity Wolfe.

She was a fine rare savage, of a type you will find nowhere now: it has been killed by the missions, the poor whites and the towns. There was a chance, at the time when those blacks were first taught to stop fighting, there was a chance then to build up a new Christianity. The right men could have built their New Jerusalem. I have seen not a little of the natives, and I have an immense faith in their character. But it is too late now. The missionaries brought them the sacrament, but

I could give you more than one instance where they brought them syphilis too. They took away everything from the natives—all those vague mysterious savage ways of mind on which their lives were conducted, often very honourably and even nobly, certainly with method, and what on earth did they give them instead? Example? No. They said they were teachers, but at every mission-station they taught them something different. I know a place where there are three missions close together, within a few miles of each other. One is Catholic, so strict that they have only a few people under their control at all. One is Protestant, and is nothing more or less than a house of ill-fame on the lines of a garden-village. There is no control of any sort and a lot of church-going. The third mission belongs to some foreign nonconformists, who change their catechism, their forms of service, even their creed continually. Well, what do the natives say——? I know there are a few *men* doing missionary work, but they are few and far between. Christianity is dead. It is a lost cause——

★ 6 ★

But I was telling you about the girl. An aboriginal, perfectly clean and perfectly beautiful. I have never seen such consummate dignity. She was rather tall and rather a light colour. She used to wear a piece of black material embroidered with grass: it was wound tightly round her body just below the breasts, and fell in straight folds to her feet. You will notice that women of taste never display their legs. The girl's name was Nhliziyombi. She was fit to be the wife of an ambassador.

Now to tell you the truth, I had been very much afraid of incurring any emotion so violent and unforeseen as that which seized me the very moment I caught sight of Nhliziyombi. From the time that I first went to Ovuzane I had been at pains to control any amorous feelings towards the natives, because I was *afraid*, unlike most of my white neighbours: even the immaculate Bloodfield had a black mistress and coloured children; and Mrs Bloodfield knew.

As soon as I had fallen in love with Nhliziyombi *I was afraid of falling in love with her.* The fear was not lessened by knowledge that she might have been sent to attract me. I had once had indisputable proof that my nearest rival in trade, a charming Jew, had sent a girl to hang about my store for a special purpose. Perhaps he hoped to lessen the efficiency of my business. Who knows? I had put Caleb, that indispensable person, in possession of the facts, and no doubt a little judicious propaganda on his part had helped to earn me my reputation and my name. It was with more than misgiving that I considered my infatuation with the ambassadress. You may laugh: but she looked like one, and she was one. She was an ambassadress of all that beauty (it might be called holiness), that intensity of the old wonderful unknown primitive African life—outside history, outside time, outside science. She was a living image of what has been killed by people like Flesher, by our obscene civilization that conquers everything. I think if you go into the question thoroughly you will find that ultimately, our civilization is obscene. It has always seemed to me to be the chief mistake of our age that we take it for granted that science is a panacea. The chief tendency of modern science has been to produce noise.

I do not propose to tell you at very great length of the affair. Why should I? It is my business. I do not even know that it developed enough to be called an affair: let me call it rather the position in which I found myself with regard to this girl.

You can guess that I suffered. Of course I could not get the girl out of my mind. I was measuring time by the rare moments when I saw her, sometimes weeks apart. Desperately I began to so fill my days that no slight opportunity was able to present itself for thoughts I desired to avoid. I would get up very early in the mornings, and busy myself with a thousand things until long after my servants were all asleep, until I could not keep my eyes open for weariness. I did not even eat my meals alone. It is perhaps a weakness, that I have never really liked to have people eating in the same room with me. You may regard it as an eccentricity: I consider it a matter of taste. The reason is simply that conversation at meals is not conversation; or, if it is, the meal is not a meal. You can't expect to get both at the same time.

Now I used to have Caleb, against all precedent, to come and sit with me at table. He was a little alarmed at first. He used to copy assiduously my behaviour, which was really very ordinary. He seemed so intent on me, so amazed at the suspicion of something unusual being in the air, that he was even more silent than usual. His natural deference was not a little disturbed when at almost every meal I would exclaim:

"Caleb, for God's sake, talk! I want words, words, words."

"Please, sir," he would ask, "what shall I say?"

"Say? Anything on earth, my son. Get your fat tongue going," I would urge, "before it dies of idleness."

He used to begin, I remember, with hesitation, but he always interested me intensely. He used to speak a very simple and deliberate, but graphic English. It was a great deal better than anything you hear spoken in E——. He often stopped, nervous, perhaps, because of the keenness with which I followed everything he said. He gave me so much food for thought that I nearly always spent half an hour with a note-book after those meals. With all my work, however, and with all my weariness at the end of it, I always found the nights were fatal. I could not sleep for the continual intrusion of that image. My dreams were scattered with the fruits of thought and emotion. My first hope on waking in the morning was always that the day might bring what I was determined that it should not bring.

I tried to sum up my position as coldly as I could. 'Where am I,' I said to myself, 'and why?' I think that afterwards reason often seems to have been a little silly, capering so energetically before the large immovable fact of love. Reason is like an urchin making a long nose at Buckingham Palace. It is nothing but sheer bravado. Love is the king, inviolable within.

What I knew fundamentally was that if I abandoned my determination I should lose my own opinion of myself. I suppose I am enough of a man to have no point as vulnerable as my own conceit.

By guarded inquiry I came to find out not a little about the girl, or rather about the circumstances surrounding her, but when it came to learning anything about her own personal character, her point of view, her friends and ambitions (even a native has friends and ambitions), I was set back by the necessity for showing not the least *intimate* interest. There was one point in particular which I ought to have known, because, when I did find it out, it was nearly too late.

A very bitter love-making. I longed to swim into a large smooth haven, and to drown the dangers of desire in the delights of content. I was like a man, a doctor, who used to be quoted as a psychological 'case': he was given to periodical fits of insanity, and used to present himself at the doors of a lunatic asylum when he felt himself seized; he used to pray that he might be received and safely harboured before he committed acts of physical violence.

I supposed myself to be in a very similar position to a monk in love with a nun. You may take it as a just enough image, and though I was not in any way ascetic I fully believe that the girl Nhliziyombi was as chaste as I was reputed to be. You can imagine, anybody can imagine, the tortures that a man suffers when he is in love against his conscience. O yes, my dear man, I had a conscience then: I have now, and I am not ashamed of it. I was in love with Nhliziyombi not only against my conscience, but against my reason; against my intellect; against my plans; *against myself*. But where do these things stand before love? I hope you will have gathered from what I have said that the vital thing was that to abandon myself to being in love with this so lovable woman would be to run counter to my vanity. That is where I want you to be quite clear. I saw that I should be sacrificing *my own opinion of myself*.

I suppose you think I mean that I was white and the girl was black. My good William Plomer, pray accept my assurance that that had nothing whatever to do with it. I am too much the humanitarian to be colour-blind. There was no question of pigment (I was in love, remember) but there appeared to be a great forbidding law, like all great forbidding laws, subcutaneous. Conscience, did I say? What had conscience to do with it? There may have been a mystery. There may have been an illusion.

As I sit here now (I breathe, as you notice, with difficulty; I know I am dying) in this cold and mothy bed; as I look on that bleak and smoky sky; as I reflect that I am dying here in E—— so long afterwards; I can almost believe that there was an illusion.—

Turbott Wolfe paused. I could hear the thudding of a football being kicked, and vague shouts that filled the winter afternoon. And in that sad and slovenly bedroom I felt very vividly the state of this man who had been torn with so many sharp emotions, true or false, and who seemed, perhaps because of them, to belong utterly to a country of calm suns and plumy flowers. The window-curtains in that room were strewn with patterned faded poppies that moved, nodding maliciously, as the curtains moved; promising an anodyne; waiting, heavy-budded, for a time when the room should be empty and obscure; waiting for a time when Turbott Wolfe, nicknamed Chastity, should be no longer there; succeeded, perhaps, by nothing but the ghost of his ecstatic voice.

★ 8 ★

—I suffered,—said Turbott Wolfe.—You see, a monk would turn to prayer. He would kneel until his back ached; he would clench his hands together until the knuckles were white; he would do penance; but he would succeed in slaughtering his passion discreetly. A neat murder with no blood-stains. Perhaps, however, there would be tell-tale finger-prints upon his soul. I wonder if monks have souls?

But how could I lose *my* pains in prayer? I am not given to prayer, except as an act of mental concentration. But I had to seek relief for my feelings, and I began (this was my stupid haven) to take violent exercise. I started cutting down trees; and tiring of that I took long aimless walks in the Native Reserve.

The third time I went out I came face to face with Nhlizi-yombi on a narrow path in the bush. It was in the morning. It was the first time I had been alone with her. She was walk-ing along in a leisurely way, playing an instrument called *makwelane*, made of a gourd with wires stretched over its mouth from the ends of a long bow of wood. You tap it with a reed, and it gives out a plaintive noise. There are only two or three notes. She was playing this thing, and singing a mel-ancholy milking-song in a low metallic voice. She did not seem surprised at meeting me (as I was confused at meeting her) but stood aside in the foliage that I might pass.

"Greeting," she said.

"Greeting," I answered. "Where are you going?"

"I am just going."

' These words were a formula, but my heart was in torment, and I could hardly keep my hands and lips from hers.

On a sudden impulse I took a gold pin that I wore in my tie, and pinned it to her clothing, where it gleamed in the sun.

"There you are," I said. "There's a present for you."

"Are you giving it?" she asked incredulously.

"It is yours."

She was alarmed at being favoured by a man she had come to know as Chastity, and exclaimed softly:

"O, white men!"

Then she ran down the path, checkered with shadows. Nor did she look back.

She is curiously innocent, I thought, frank, delicate. Is it truly because I am afraid of myself that I am afraid of loving her? Is it not perhaps that I am afraid of her? How could I touch, perhaps to injure, that frail divine humanity, or human divinity? I could not give myself reasons, but suspected that I was cheating myself. They were disarming, those wide Egyptian eyes. No, I said to myself, I dare not touch her.

I did not see Nhliziyombi again for a week. There was a noisy crowd in the shop, and I was busy serving with Caleb. The girl wandered in with others, and was swept away on a torrent of chatter.

I gave up walking abroad from Ovuzane for fear of meeting the girl, and sought to drown my struggles in music. I worked out every shade of emotion over and over again, improvising sometimes on the violin, and sometimes on the piano, which stood in the large room called the studio.

One very clear moonlight night I was sitting up late making variations on a persistent inevitable theme. I came abruptly to an end; closed the piano; turned out the light; and went out, meaning to take a turn in the cool night air before going to bed. All at once, as I closed the door behind me, I heard a choking sound in the shadows somewhere near at hand. I was more puzzled than alarmed. Imagine my amazement when I found Caleb Msomi, the storeman, leaning against the wall with his head down; his hands clapping faintly together; and the whole of his large frame shaken with those small dry sobs that indicate a very poignant grief.

At first I thought he was drunk, and I remembered with a shock that I had never seen him drunk. (It wouldn't have been like him. He was nearly as steady as a machine, and wanted little watching.)

I approached him quietly, and in a state of utter bewilderment, calling his name softly.

He looked up sharply when he heard me, with a shamefaced expression.

"Caleb," I asked, "why are you weeping?"

He paused a moment before he admitted, still choking with queer little sobs, like a child after much crying:

"Your music made me sad."

I was never so surprised in my life. The native character——! To find such a depth of tenderness in a sober, an almost too respectable person like Caleb, took me unawares. White people think they are so acute about the native character: pooh, they know nothing about it. You will hear them in Africa, those especially who have had to do with the administration of natives, you will hear them boast:

"I have worked with natives for thirty-two years, and I don't pretend to understand them now——"

But it is a lie. You can see it written on their silly red faces. They *do* pretend to understand. And almost before you have time to sneer at them in your heart an exposition begins:

"Of course, they are just like children."

Or:

"Of course, they are just like animals."

How penetrating are the eyes of people who talk like that, how very hawk-like. Why, they can't see even so far as the ends of their own noses. . . .

I had grown tired of chopping trees; walking was dangerous; with music I had harrowed my poor servant's feelings—

where was I to turn to hide my own harrowed feelings? I began to keep a record of emotion in the form of a journal. Of course it could not be as personal as music, but I shall give you a few readings from it in order to show you various lines of thought that I must have taken.

Turbott Wolfe's diary had a worn black cover. He took it from a table at the side of his bed, and held it in his thin hands while he was talking.

* 9 *

—By the way,—said Turbott Wolfe,—this journal was kept without any punctuation except that afforded by the days. It was an experiment. One punctuates with the voice.

I began it in the winter, which is a rare time of year at Ovuzane. We used even at times to get frost in the long starry nights. The days were short and sweet. The days were solemn. There was very little wind at that time of year. The sun rose late, very large and slow, and swam across the quiet unexpectant days. There would be long shadows until nearly noon, and the afternoons were all long-shadowed too. And it would be night.

In winter nights at Ovuzane the stars would prick you like pins. You have heard about the stars seen from Africa, and now you have heard about the stars seen from Ovuzane.

Do you believe in astrology? I do.

The winter there is a time for burning the grass, which is apt to get too coarse and tough for the cattle if you don't keep it down with fire. Ovuzane is the place for grass fires: when a whole range of mountains is violet-coloured with cold, in the upper air, the moment after the sun has set, there is nothing so wonderful as to see one solitary peak inflamed with fire and crowned with smoke, in that uncanny icy upper air, fifty miles from where you stand.

I ask you to note that the first entry in this journal was made on an evening when the mountains of Ovuzanyana presented just such an aspect. I can remember it clearly. The date was

July 24

To-night I see fires like small worms upon the furthest mountains there blinded with heat no doubt women and men are beating out the flames with boughs so at the moment I view objectively the part I am playing aware of its dangers.

That gives you, as accurately as possible, I think, in words, my state of mind at that moment. Music might have been far more exact, but there is so much pain in music: that was why I chose to use words instead. I planted words round my emotion as you plant trees round a house: they draw attention to the white walls of truth within, which at the same time they partly conceal. I do not intend to read you every entry that was made. I am giving you short passages here and there, those that will emphasize the truth.

Some days later Nhliziyombi came to the shop when it was empty but for Caleb and myself. Caleb served her, I watched her. I noticed especially the *kindness* of her nature: she showed in a very marked way that almost aggressive mildness and courtesy, sincere and instinctive, that you only find in certain savages that have never happened on some

God-forsaken missionary. I had a slight and ordinary conversation with her. She was delightfully shy. After she had gone I was in a torment—soothed with hope and pleasure, and shaken with a kind of impotent anger. It was a bitter afternoon. I wrote in the journal:

JULY 28

Fresh from you I am dazed the wintry sun declining in a thin wind I walked among the mango trees lighting cigarettes under my coat I am dazed the smoke dispersing.

Having seen her again, I wrote on

JULY 30

It is I that triumph and I that am bound captive to the wheels exultant.

Isn't it ludicrous to consider that it is possible for a man's vanity to be bound captive to the wheels exultant of his triumphing heart? It seems utterly absurd. Your civilization may be obscene, but it is remarkably intricate.

I was amused at the way Turbott Wolfe said 'your civilization.' It was no more mine than his: in fact, it was less mine than his. But I thought it would be unkind to remind the slave of the tyrant, and said no word.

—During the following week—said Turbott Wolfe—we

reached the only point of intimacy in the matter. I don't see why I should give you any details of the interview: after all, it was my business.

There was a banana-grove about a mile from the house. That was the place where I happened on Nhliziyombi, not quite by accident, on a warm clear afternoon. I told her that I loved her intensely, but that my name forbade me to go any further than a confession of my love. I felt a coward. She was puzzled and alarmed at first, but warmed into sympathy. She took my head for a moment between her lean brown hands. We sat in the banana-grove, frankly content, without moving or uttering a word for more than an hour.

It was one of the saddest, happiest days of my life.

I wrote in the journal:

AUGUST 3

To-day was a city drunk with success I went through it upon wheels the cortege the thoroughfares the shouting crowds and midday was the many-windowed turning-point where the clamour was loudest (I was mad with joy at the ecstasy of your silence) but the outer streets were empty and to-night the conqueror is desolate in the luxury of his hollow palace.

On a certain evening a few days later I could not prevent myself waiting at the foot of the mango-orchard to watch a path along which I expected Nhliziyombi to pass. Nor was I disappointed. With a great black earthenware pot on her head she was crossing a stream in the valley. As she went up the opposite slope I could see that she wore a long tight crimson gown, girded up under the arms, and falling to her ankles. She walked more gracefully than anybody I have seen before or since. I watched her ascending slowly, and when she entered a grove of trees at the top of the hill her crimson dress went black, and she suddenly disappeared.

As a potential lover I knew at once that she had disappeared for ever. I wrote in the journal:

AUGUST 6

It seems that whenever I see you it is less of a greeting than a parting now I come from seeing you going I saw you in the distance entering the wood hesitate dark among the dark trunks disappear and the trees that had been finely arched buoyant on the slope concealing you took on at once a heaviness the summits of foliage weighing upon the trees because of the numbness of their density with night ebbing into the sky I was all at once aware of a bright line of fire leaping along the skyline above the dusk.

I turned home that chill and limpid evening melting with melancholy. All the stars came out and pricked me like pins. I saw the white walls of my house. . . .

★ 10 ★

One day I asked Caleb:

"What has happened to that girl Nhliziyombi, who used to be here quite often?"

"She has gone, sir, to be married to her cousin at Hlohloko. It is far from here. They have been betrothed for half a year. She loves her man, who has rejected three girls to marry her, but all the parents are angry. It is not our custom for cousins to marry one another. She is a kind girl. She will be a very good wife. Very good. The man is wild, but he will become a lamb. I have made sure that we shall not lose Nhliziyombi as a customer. A group of friends will assist her to purchase the wedding-goods at our store, and I shall not fail to induce them to buy more than they mean to."

The girl had actually been engaged to a man she loved during the whole time that I had been interested in her. She might well have shown alarm that day under the broad-leaved banana trees.

While I was busy with stock-taking at the end of August I had two anonymous letters. One was from a native:

Dear Mr Wolfe,

I am speaking for my native people. We see that you are in sympathy with us: and we are glad. We know also that you are true to your name of Chastity, and we are full of joy. We hope that you will not be afraid to help us in the political world. We know that a good man is greater than governments. We pray that you will carry on the good work you have begun.—We are, your obedient servants,

THOSE WHO KNOW

This was very noble. The other letter was in a deplorable style, presumably from Flesher:

You had better be careful. You think people have no ears or eyes. Your tricks are known. If you go on hobnobbing with niggers there are others besides the Government that will get their knife into you. There are other White people in Lembuland besides you. You call yourself a White man: but you behave like a ——. Look out!

I will admit that I found this disturbing. I did not feel in the least afraid of Flesher and his kind, but the suggestion that the Government might disapprove of me set me thinking. My relations with the authorities, I reflected, had always been perfectly smooth. As I was trading under a special licence from the Government, on what were supposed to be unusually favourable terms, I had always been assiduously careful to keep within my rights. The first thing I did was to inspect with care the list of conditions governing my licence 'to occupy the trading-station of Ovuzane for the purpose of lawful trading with the aboriginal inhabitants of Native Reserve No. 61, commonly known as the Ovuzane Reserve, in accordance with the conditions hereinafter set forth.' I had read all this verbiage before, but I was astounded once more (one always is astounded on reading these official documents) at the number of things I mustn't do. I felt like a very small new boy at a very large old school, who takes the trouble to read the rules, and finding that he must do this; that he must not do that; that he must not talk in such a place at such a time; and who, finding that he is forbidden to make use of catapults, air-guns, stones or bread-pellets, begins at last to wonder what he is really free to do.

There were a great many clauses in my licence. Typically, I must not, I found, make any objection to the 'laying down' (I should have called it 'setting up') 'of telegraphic or telephonic communication, or the establishment of any other form or method of transmitting or conveying, or of causing to be transmitted or conveyed, any communications whatsoever,' either in, under, or over my land. You know the sort of thing. I suppose all governments are alike in that way. I found that I must not keep, or even cause or encourage to be kept, a bar or a brothel: but as I had never had the slightest ambition to found any institution on those lines, this injunction left me rather cold. But of course governments have to protect themselves against the sort of people you always find swarming in colonies—people whose first idea *would* be to run a bar or a brothel on the sly, and who would use the proceeds to have all their daughters taught to ill-treat really quite good pianos, and to pick bread-and-butter (so thin that it always breaks) with the left forefinger and thumb off what I believe are called d'oyleys: people who would aim at making their sons dentists and lawyers, in a vague hope that a practice of mucking about with the insides of other people's mouths and private affairs would turn them into little gentlemen. Those are the people who have to be taught not to interfere with those telegraph-lines which will never be laid down, or set up.

The only clause which held my attention was one which ran something like this:

'The licencee is not to interfere or intervene in any way or to cause interference or intervention of any kind or description whatsoever or to encourage or to provoke in any way any form of interference or intervention in any questions, matters, arrangements, laws, rules, agreements, settlements or disputes arising from, or pertaining to, or concerned or in any way connected with any political or tribal affairs whatsoever, pertaining to or in any way concerning the aboriginal inhabitants, commonly called natives, of Reserve No. 61, commonly known as the Ovuzane Reserve; or of any other reserve, settlement, or location; or of any other area whatsoever outside such reserve, settlement, or location, within the boundaries of the province of Lembuland, the GOVERNMENT to be the sole arbiter of what does or does not constitute interference or intervention on the part of the licencee.'

I read that offending against this clause I might be liable to

three months' notice; to cancellation of my licence; to con-
fiscation of buildings and improvements; and in an extreme
case to a heavy fine. This was all very alarming, but I had
never thought twice about political interference. 'Hobnobbing with niggers', the anonymous letter had said. Well, I
used to treat them as equals, not entirely for the sake of trade,
but because it charmed me to do so; the natives responded to
kindness.

Now I was so incensed by this disgusting letter (filthier in
contrast with the other that came by the same post); by the
cumbrous wordy restrictions some oily bureaucrat had attempted to place on the warm heart of any human that saw
the black man first not as a black but as a man; so distressed
by the steely intangible barrier that had been between me
and Nhliziyombi; that I was almost driven on the hot impulse of the moment to that very political interference so
expressly forbidden.

Just as before I had felt the overwhelming influence of the
natives, so now I felt that there was no escape from the poor
whites like Flesher and his kind, like the Government, like
the rulers and taskmasters of the unfortunate natives. I had
thought them petty before: now they seemed unclean. This
was an impression that went deeper as the result of succeeding
events. It was the final and lasting impression.

2

★ I ★

MY nearest white neighbour was a man I hardly ever saw. He rented a farm from old Nordalsgaard's mission (it was a piece of land grabbed long ago by the almighty Klodquist), a farm that lay a few miles to the left of the road from Ovuzane to Hlanzeni. The name of the farm was Silver Hill, and the name of the farmer was Schwerdt. He was a German, aged something between thirty and forty. Very fair he was, and meanly built, with an awkward square-shouldered stoop. He had pale untrustworthy eyes slightly protruding beneath shaggy eyebrows, a short nose and a long receding chin. As he stooped he held his head low, and his watery eyes always looked up at you with a peculiar expression of cunning. A ragged yellow moustache concealed his nasty mouth. He, too, was unclean. Shifty.

I had always disliked him. His reputation was even more unsavoury than his appearance, and he seemed to have no character at all. He used to do jobbing building work at Aucampstroom when he could get it, and was not too lazy to take it. I suppose he had to do something to supplement an income that certainly could not accrue from idling and drinking on the farm—unless he was engaged there dealing in illicit liquor, which was not unlikely.

I had once employed Schwerdt, by way of experiment, on some small job when I first went to Ovuzane, but he had been such a bad workman, such a slovenly slipshod workman, that I had been forced to drive him out with a stick.

As you know, my temper has never been seraphic, and when I am greatly worried and unsettled, as I had happened to be at that time, it does not improve. I need hardly say that there was no mutual forgiveness. He always hated me, because he knew I had everything he lacked and everything that it was impossible for him to acquire, or even to have thrown to him. People in such a position as Schwerdt's are apt to be bitter. He was a waster himself, but I believe his father had been worse. The old man had come out to Africa as a missionary in days long past, but finding that he could not collect money and women quite fast enough had deserted his pulpit for a counter. He had, indeed, attempted to trade on the very site that I was afterwards to occupy. He failed, old Schwerdt, they tell me, because of his brutal treatment of the natives. He was murdered by a native woman to whom he had given a disease that shall be nameless. Young Schwerdt seemed a true son of his father. He had married a young Dutchwoman from the back of beyond. She was gross, but handsome in an evil unhealthy way, with a very full, very loose mouth. I only saw her once or twice, but I had found it hard to be even civil to her, because it was so unpleasantly obvious that she was unaware of the uses of soap.

Schwerdt and his wife had a very bad name with the natives, who were afraid of the man on account of his aggressive temper. They had done me a good deal of harm at the beginning, setting natives against me in various ways. After a time I came to note that Silver Hill was becoming a rendezvous for natives known to be of bad character. Silver Hill must be a house of ill-fame. I could learn nothing definite. There were murmurings. There were tears. There was silence.

Late one afternoon, when I was about to close the store, an

evil old native came to me with a parcel, a grimy shapeless parcel, that he desired me to deliver to Schwerdt.

"O, go to hell," I said. "What is it?"

The old man screwed up his eyes. He was a very old man. His hands were shaking.

"O, sir," he whined, "it is just something of his."

"Why don't you deliver your rotten parcels yourself?"

"It is too far for me to walk. Sir, I am an old man. It is far, very far. Once I was young," he mumbled.

"O, very well," I said, for the sake of peace. I sent a small boy, one of my own servants, off to Schwerdt's farm with the parcel. I went to bed early, and I must have just fallen asleep, when I was woken up by Caleb, who came to tell me that the boy had returned and particularly desired to be allowed to see me at once. I was very annoyed at being disturbed, and meaning to scold the boy for returning at such an hour, I told Caleb to call him in. But as soon as I saw his young face, profoundly distressed, I changed my intention. I sat up, leaning on my elbow, and asked gently:

"Boy, why did you not stay at Silver Hill until morning, as I ordered you before you left?"

"Sir," he answered in a childish voice grown thick with emotion, "I arrived there at sunset. But when I approached the house my brother Frans, who is working there as a cook, came down the path to meet me, very angrily, with a whip in his hand, and asked me what I meant by coming there at all. I tried to give him the parcel for the white man, but he knocked it out of my hand. Then he lifted his whip, and began to swear and curse at me, saying he would give me a beating if I did not make off at once. By this time it was dark, and people do not like to be out in the night, so, although I was frightened of his anger, I asked him for a place to sleep.

This seemed to enrage him more than ever, and I began to explain that you, sir, had commanded me to sleep there to-night. At this moment I heard strange noises in the white man's house at the top of the path. These noises seemed to drive my brother mad, and he shouted, 'Don't you know that this is the white man's house, you little ——! How can I let you sleep in the white man's house? Get away!' At this moment he began to whip me, but I escaped, and fled straight home."

"But I am sorry to say, sir," he added, "that I have brought the parcel back again by mistake."

"You have done well, boy," I said, "to try and obey your master's orders, but it was wrong to bring back the parcel. Where is it now? You may give it to me, and then get some food, and go to bed."

The parcel was brought, and Caleb retired with the boy.

Certain old suspicions were renewed in me. I could not sleep. I reflected on the noises that the boy said he had heard proceeding from the house, and on the extraordinary behaviour of his brother Frans, so inconsistent with native character. Finally, on a sudden impulse, I got out of bed, lit my lamp, and opened the parcel. I don't think I am the sort of person who is given to opening other people's parcels habitually, but on this occasion I had a fixed idea that I must see what was inside. I knew that the contents of the parcel would tell me what was going on at Silver Hill. I proved to be right.

The parcel contained certain illegal articles of commerce of a kind that I have never seen outside Africa. I was aghast.

I felt unclean from contact with the parcel, and it was a long time before I could get to sleep.

Directly after I had opened the store, very early the following morning, Caleb came and announced that Schwerdt was sitting outside on his horse, waiting for a word with me.

"Give Mr Schwerdt my compliments," I said, busy measuring a piece of purple material, "and tell him I should be glad to see him in here."

Colony or no colony, I didn't feel prepared to be jawed from the saddle by a man like that.

Schwerdt came in with an insolent air, his head down and his eyes up, and in a low voice demanded:

"Why should you send your blasted niggers to spy on me?"

I must confess that I became a little heated. I said:

"Get out of my shop, you filthy monkey! Go back and fetch the manners you have left at home, before you come and presume to talk rubbish to me. I sent my servant, if you want to know, to give you a parcel of yours, which I may tell you is now in my possession."

Schwerdt's face took on a ghastly colour, and he blurted out:

"I have come to fetch it."

"Too late," I said. "I regret that it is now impossible for me to deliver it to you. You see, I happen to know what it contains."

He looked at me for an instant. Then he took a chequebook out of his pocket and laid it on the counter. It was not from shame, but fear, that his hands were shaking.

"If you'll say nothing about it——" he said thickly.

"No," I said, "that's no use. This is hardly a matter of money."

There was nothing more to be said. Schwerdt went away.

As for me, I went over to Hlanzeni to tell Nordalsgaard what I thought of his tenant.

"I didn't know it was as bad as that," he said. "I am thankful that he's leaving this part of the country."

"Leaving?"

"He gave us notice some time ago. He is due to leave at the end of this month. Ah, the unfortunate natives——"

We consoled ourselves with coffee from a brass pot of burnished antiquity, nor were we indifferent to Miss Rosa Grundso's sweet Norwegian confections. But when I was alone again with my own white walls at home, and when I was alone in my gloomy tropical treeful garden, I felt sick. I don't think it is an exaggeration to say that the house at Silver Hill had seen the most abandoned exhibition of the beast in man that I had ever heard of. I had got incontestable proof that the Schwerdts had mixed up with their filthiness various manifestations of the worst and most degraded aspect of certain old African customs connected with sorcery. When you remember that it has usually been considered impossible for white people to get at all in touch with that sort of thing, you will understand that I had reason to be profoundly shocked. Perhaps I am absurdly sensitive? You know me well enough to judge.

Unclean, I said to myself, unclean. Now, at the first opportunity, I would 'interfere or intervene' on behalf of the natives. I felt that I did not care whether it should be openly or secretly. I felt ready to sacrifice a very great deal in order to preserve for the natives a little of the quality that had been almost lost to them before the combined ruthlessness of the poor white and the missionary and the official. The unfortunate natives, as Nordalsgaard called them, had had their bodies and souls exploited too long. Frankness, innocence, dignity, *quality*—were they to go down before the affected mincing tread of Flesher's canary legs? before the sub-bestial unimaginable indecency of a blear-eyed snotty-nosed Teuton?

★ 2 ★

The Schwerdts went to live at the Cape, a long way from Lembuland. Not many months later I read in the paper that Mrs Schwerdt had been struck dead by lightning, a divine visitation. I cut this obituary notice from a contemporary South African paper:

Van Honk

In Fond Memory of Wesseliena Lily van Honk, our Darling Rosebud, suddenly snatched to Jesus on 14th November, 19—.

"All there is to answer when we call your name,
Is your photo, lovey Lily, in the frame."

Gone, but not forgotten.
This notice inserted by her ever-sorrowing parents; her brothers Dirk, Barend, Louie, and Jan; and her sisters Gretel, Lulu, and Dotta. Also by her heartbroken hubby Heinrich Schwerdt. Also by Cousin Cossie, of Aucampstroom, Lembuland.

'Cousin Cossie' was the lady I had once happened on as I left the Fotheringhays, a very worthy cousin to Mrs Schwerdt.

I called on the Fotheringhays now for diversion from the violence of my thoughts. Mrs Fotheringhay wore a white rose, drooping (I suppose with disappointment at finding itself pinned to so unromantic a bosom) among the souvenirs of soup and grape-like buttons on her perennial black dress. Her husband had been writing a twelve-page letter to somebody in England on a question of heraldry. There was a fire blazing up the chimney, that hot afternoon. The screens of scarlet baize were immaculate. The cat was on the mat, speculating on its own affairs. *Punch* was on a side-table. On the piano was a vase of violets. On the sideboard I noticed three cruets, two empty bottles, a pair of gloves, a bird's nest, some roots, an old Georgian silver candlestick, a dead moth, a copy of the *Daily Mail Year Book* ten years old, and a copy of *Mr Britling Sees It Through*.

Mrs Fotheringhay said they had no servants. Alice was away, and the boy she had told to come in her place until she returned had come once and had then been summoned by his prospective bride's maternal uncle to help to settle a dispute about somebody else's cattle. It *was* difficult.

"And I believe the wretch took two forks with him, too. I don't like to think that he took them, but when Alice went away they were here——"

"Mr Wolfe doesn't want to hear all that," said Mr Fotheringhay. "He has troubles of his own, I expect."

"I was only telling him," said Mrs Fotheringhay ineffectually.

We had tea. Out of the window I could see two little unwashed white girls, four or five years old, mocking at a drunken native in the street.

"That is why this is going to be a black man's country," I suggested to the rector.

He shrugged his shoulders very very slightly.

"I suppose one has to put up with it," he said. "We have to put up with a good deal. The doctor says Mrs Fotheringhay ought to have three months at the sea. I suppose he says that just because he knows we can't afford it, and has to say something to look as if he was earning his fee. Mrs Fotheringhay go away indeed! Why, she hasn't been out of this house for six months."

"My father," said Mrs Fotheringhay, "once took a house at Bognor for the summer. It *was* beautiful. Do you know Bognor?"

I had to confess that I did not know Bognor, but I knew that it was time for me to return home. They were kindness itself, these two beautiful Fotheringhays, these charming innocuous anachronisms. I reflected, driving home to Ovuzane, that although they had spent nearly all their lives in Africa, they had never begun to think of Africa. The rector himself must have noticed where he was, and I suppose he concluded that they must put up with it. But as for Mrs Fotheringhay, she had clung tenaciously to the past: the older she got, it was plain, the more vivid it became. For her there was nothing so real in the world as the warm sweet savour of the wallflowers that had been growing under the drawing-room windows in Surrey in the early 'seventies: the scent was in her nostrils still. It was still in her small white nostrils. Nothing in Africa could match the inviolable memory of the heavy intoxicating clusters of lilac, wet with rain and honey, bowed down and odorous on a vanished English lawn. And there was that prodigious father with long perfumed whiskers; a double-breasted waistcoat; a habit of taking houses (or castles) for the summer at places so far distant from one another as Drumdoodle and Bognor; that father who had once given ninety guineas for a horse; that father who conjured apples from abroad (or was it Yorkshire?) into a massive and elegant dining-room that had a curious compound smell. A smell it was that had seemed to the future Mrs Fotheringhay the most important and distinguished in the world: it suggested the ghosts of wine and fruit and tobacco; of peaches and punch; of warm ink, letters unwritten, beautiful books unopened; of a marble clock that presided on the mantelpiece; of servants in livery; of domestic tragedy; of Darwin and Disraeli; and of distinguished visitors. It was a smell that might accurately be called Victorian. And perhaps Mrs Fotheringhay might accurately have been called Victorian, too.

She had lived, incredible Englishwoman, for fifteen years in Aucampstroom without noticing that Aucampstroom existed. It only belonged for her to that shadowy subconscious dream-world that is peopled with the ghosts of what we feel deep down in our hearts, and not of what we think we feel.

Alice, with her frightful smile, was a tall uncanny ghost; and so, I have no doubt, was the doctor; and Alfredson, the coloured tradesman who guaranteed Mr Fotheringhay's stipend, must have been, too; and so, no doubt, was I. Mrs Fotheringhay saw us all with the same eyes that the fish, staring palely through green water and plate-glass, uses to inspect the ridiculous visitors to the aquarium. Mr Fotheringhay alone could have belonged, in any sense, to the same world as his wife's father's whiskers in 1870 or 1860: but even her impression of him would be fading now before the warm immediate savour of the gillyflowers. . . .

★ 3 ★

I find myself—said Turbott Wolfe—in the studio at Ovuzane. I am at home, but I am taken with a mood of abysmal sadness. The air is thunderous (it is late afternoon), charged with electricity, with violence. I have always been sensitive to weather conditions, and I, too, am charged with electricity, with a flowing current, more suave than threatening, of potential violence. I am at the window to watch the approaching storm. The sky is darkly overcast, blue and tortuous, undershot with a few flung rays of the westering sun, now invisible. There is thunder. Lightning. The last rays of the sun are lemon-coloured.

I am admiring my avenue of tree-ferns: all at once the wide extended leaves are creamed and writhing like waves of the sea, before an onslaught of wind. And under them a figure, with head bowed and body muffled against the storm, is rapidly approaching; it is a figure as significant as an omen; it is a supernatural figure; coming under the agonized tree-ferns, out of mystery, to me.

At first I thought it was a woman: no, it was not a woman. Where had I seen this man before? Surely it was Caleb's cousin, Zachary Msomi, that I had met at old Frank d'Elva-dere's. "He is going to be a parson," old Frank had said. I remembered shaking hands with him, full of defiant thoughts about my white acquaintances.

Zachary came up the road with the delicacy and dignity of a king. Too great a breadth he had of chest and shoulders, holding himself as though the world were his (albeit he battled with the wind), narrow-middled, hipless, with muscular arms and legs, and long lean hands. His face was a trifle malicious, but handsome; his whole carriage dominated by a sharp aquiline nose, strange in a Lembu, got no doubt from an alien forefather, some lord in Barbary.

But he was not coming to me. He saluted me, passing round the side of the house to the servants' quarters. Heavy drops of rain were falling: thicker and faster they came until the ear was oppressed with the sombre rumour of a downpour. As for me, I walked up and down the studio. I touched with my hand a piece of sculpture, my own work, that stood upon a pedestal in a recess; that had been admired: I caressed it as though it were human. My eyes found pictures on the wall, and a chest against it where others were stored. There were the drawers of a bureau full of manuscripts—prose, verse, music. And all about me were my tools and mediums and instruments—a chisel, a camera, a spade, a pen, a piano. I thought of the unfortunate Tyler-Harries, fresh from the keen intellectual air of London, who had warmed me with praise; who had declared he would make my name at a blow; who had gone down, uncoffined, and more than a little drunk on raw cane-spirit, in company with a lady of colour, down, down, with only bubbles to his funeral, down to the uttermost depths of the sea. Now he was associated in my mind with a whole host of others. He was with those who had been broken or beaten or besotted with the almighty violence of Africa, that violence which was the tropical thunderstorm raging on the roof; which was the grace of Zachary; the beauty of Nhliziyombi; and even the trustworthiness of Caleb. I could see plainly that Tyler-Harries was in the same category as the Schwerdts, whose beastliness had been turned against them by witchcraft: as the Fotheringhays, who had been drugged with Africa, so that their brains could not cope with it, caressing only the ghosts of memory and tradition: as Flesher and Bloodfield and their kind, whose vulgarity only emphasized the colossal disastrous significance of their background: as Nordalsgaard, whose conquests were like land reclaimed for a time, and afterwards choked with weeds. It was not the same with d'Elvadere, the voluptuous pioneer, who was his own master: it had not been the same with the *voortrekkers*—only with their descendants, the poor whites, broken by colour, climate and disease. Even the vast fabric of government, the preposterous structure of officialdom, had been set up to conceal and control what could not be hidden or ordered: it was denied by the mere existence of that which it sought to restrict. I thought of the anonymous letter and my licence, and I felt increasingly bitter. I felt also a sudden fear that I too might be sacrificed, a victim to the inexorable Mumbo-Jumbo: and I swore proudly to myself that Africa should never master me. I felt a sudden impulse to swift and dangerous political action: Zachary, somewhere at the back of the house, should be a pivot. He had seemed an omen; he should be a tool, or a symbol, or a weapon.

I had begun by feeling sad and ended by feeling violent. The rain poured down incessantly, clamorous with thunder, seared with lightning. Ah, would that it might batter down this studio, this churchlike temple of my past, flood it and spoil it, that I might step forth free with Zachary and Caleb, with moral violence, to conquer Africa!

I thought of what Van Gogh once said about Christ:

". . . *artiste plus grand que tous les artistes, dédaignant et le marbre et l'argile et la couleur, travaillant en chair vivante.*"

Without seeking to put myself on the level of Christ, yet I too would work in living flesh.

★ 4 ★

On the following morning, which was Sunday, I felt a wish to have a look at the scene of the Schwerdt affair. When

I left home there wasn't a cloud in the sky. The sun was hot and the air was steamy. A fine torrid morning; but a light breeze began to blow, and walking became delightful. As I came to Silver Hill it must have been nearly noon, and the silver grass (from which the place took its name) that covered the hill like hair, like fire, was long and wavy in the sun and wind, glittering like glass, glossy like silk. On the summit of the hill there was a garden, dark with cypresses and firs, the shelter of the house from eyes raised up; but as I drew near the dingy wall and shuttered windows could be seen among the branches, and the square sloping roof of thatch. Passing through a wicket-gate in the barbed-wire fence that surrounded the garden I noticed that the earth at my feet was a vivid terra-cotta colour, washed into plastic mud by last night's rain, and bearing the impress of tiny birds' feet. There was a native that I knew from the Hlanzeni mission acting as caretaker, and I asked him for the key, saying that I wanted to see the house.

"O," he said, "there's a white man in the house already."

He pointed to the ground. In the mud were the marks of a booted foot, criss-crossed fantastically by the little birds' tracks.

"But who is it?" I asked.

"I think it is a new missionary who has come lately to Hlanzeni."

The front door was open. And so was the door of the dining-room. In the middle of the floor the man was kneeling. He had his back to me. He was wearing a long black coat. I stood in the doorway thoroughly surprised, too surprised to say any word at all. In a moment the man got up and turned round. He looked at me quite calmly (he must have heard me come in) and said:

"How d'you do?"

Then he stooped down quite deliberately and brushed with his hand the knees of his trousers, a little dusty from the deserted floor where he had been at prayer. We shook hands. I said:

"I hope I am not intruding, but I have a psychological interest in this house, and it looks as though you have too."

"Then we're both intruders," he answered. "My name's Friston. I'm supposed to be a missionary. I've just come lately to the Hlanzeni mission. This is only my third Sunday here, in fact. Instead of church I came for a long walk this morning: I haven't been well, so I thought it would do me more good. I've really come the deuce of a way. I had some tea right away at a farm up there in the hills. A man called Bloodfield. He thought I was mad. He was full of abuse. (I hope he's not a friend of yours?) He abused everything he could lay his tongue to, except himself. A frightful person. He told me very dark stories about this place, so I came on here out of curiosity. I found a native outside who let me in."

He paused.

"You were probably surprised to see me praying? The truth is, I found some obscene pictures in here. I've been burning them. There are the frames on the table, there are the ashes on the floor. I've been praying for the unfortunates that had the making of them—that's why you found me on my knees. Mind you, I don't know that I believe in prayer. And between ourselves, don't you see, although I am a priest I have my own views about God. In this case it was simply an impulse. I had to clear the air."

This young priest, I thought, spoke with an unusual directness. In his attitude to life I saw (I was pleased to see) a reflection of myself. Vanity. Or perhaps excitement at getting in touch with a point of view something removed from the usual point of view to be found in Lembuland. Perhaps this Friston seemed especially frank in contrast with most of my white neighbours, people whose eyes and thoughts were shifty; and whose speech came from mouths filled with venom instead of spittle; people like the very Bloodfield he had just seen, who had thought this emphatic and winning young man mad.

"You're very refreshing," I said. "It's rather a shock to find anybody like you here. I'm not used to people who are in any way frank or open. The farmers of Ovuzanyana (of whom our mutual friend Bloodfield is a specimen) and the inhabitants of Aucampstroom don't generally have much feeling, and their knees are as little worn with prayer as their hearts with charity. In this part of the world we only look for anything like spontaneity in the natives."

"O, Lord," said Friston, "are they as bad as that?"

"They are," I said.

"I suspected it: but of course I didn't come here for their sake. A missionary is supposed to devote himself to the natives, and I think I had rather do so. The idea is that I should relieve old Nordalsgaard a little. He's getting on, and I expect he's finding life more of a struggle than he cares to admit. Now that I've met you, the prospect of living here takes on a new face. We're friends already."

"You honour me too much," I declared pompously. Perhaps I was flattered, and nothing is lost by a little flourish of courtesy.

"No speeches," said the missionary, with a grin.

"Look here," I said, "let's go outside and talk. It's much better outside."

We found a place to sit under the dark trees in the garden. Over the flowers (mostly ragged dahlias) we had a view of the Ovuzanyana mountains, with Bloodfield's house visible high up, like a cork floating on waves. We began talking, like all white men in Africa, about the natives.

"Now," I said, "you're a missionary. Can you tell me what on earth your sort of religion has to do with these natives? Do you honestly think that Christianity can ever touch them? It's like giving them a slap in the face, and hoping they will be branded for life."

"I know what you mean," Friston answered, "but I think Christianity's a useful weapon. The German missionaries make it pay five per cent. They know how to do things. They've got brains. To be quite honest with you, I'm only a parson myself because of a kind of family tradition. I never feel that I have much freedom: most parsons are fools (my mother says they all are), and they're the worst gossips in the world, especially about each other. But, you see, for eight generations without a break one of us has been in the Church. I've only got two brothers: the eldest insisted on going into the Army, and the other's epileptic, so I had no choice. My father's Bishop of Crotchester, but my mother was a chorus-girl: her father was a country parson, and I always rag her for coming back to the Church again, after being on the Stage. She has always harped at me since my job was first settled: 'O, Rupert, do get some guts into it.' That's just what I want to do. I only tell you all this because I don't want you to think I am the usual humbug, going about with my collar back-to-front and my tongue in my cheek. I don't think England would hold me. That's why I'm here. I happened to overhear my father being advised to 'send him out for a bit to the mission-field: that'll tame him down'. But it won't.

O no, don't you believe it. On the contrary, I am only just beginning to get worked up."

"What exactly are you getting worked up towards?" I asked.

"It's rather soon to tell you," he answered, with a pause. "Do you mind having your breath taken away?"

"My dear man," I said, "after living for a time at Ovuzane, with eyes and ears open, my breath cannot be taken away. I am become the complete Colonial. They always say that Colonials, like Americans, are incapable of expressing surprise or admiration. I suppose they see so many strange things always at hand. I defy you to surprise me."

"Credo," he announced in a voice of awe, prodding the ground with his forefinger, and speaking as distinctly as an oracle. "I believe that the white man's day is over. Anybody can see plainly that the world is quickly and inevitably becoming a coloured world. I do not assert yet that miscegenation should be actually encouraged, but I believe that it is the missionary's work now, and the work of any white man in Africa worth his salt, to prepare the way for the ultimate end. Let us take the native, and instead of yapping to him about Jesus Christ and Noah's Ark, let us tell him about himself, not in relation to Hebrew folk-lore, but in relation to himself and to the white man. I think that's where my work lies."

His face was thrust forward. His eyes were fixed on me. His lips were set. It was the face of a prophet.

We sat in silence for a time.

"I agree with you," I said, "but although you are vague about details I don't see how you'll reconcile all this with Nordalsgaard and his ideas."

"I shall not try. He's going to retire. He's going back to Norway within six months. He can't get anybody but me to take over his blooming mission. I propose to take it over in my own way."

"You'll have a merry time," I said. "That mission's got a bad name."

"I can see that," said Friston.

"I must tell you a little story," I said, "that I had from a charming old man called d'Elvadere, who has many stories. There's a coloured teacher, Olaf Shaw, who's supposed to be Nordalsgaard's son, and used to work at Hlanzeni. Now d'Elvadere was once at the mission-house on business. As he rode away he heard Shaw conducting some sort of Sunday-school in the church. He stopped his horse at a window and listened a moment out of curiosity. They were discussing the parable of The Foolish Virgins. A native girl of about fifteen or sixteen, with the figure of a woman of forty, held up her hand. 'Please, teacher,' she was heard to say, 'what *is* a virgin?' A titter of laughter ran through the class. D'Elvadere caught Shaw's answer: 'Albertina, don't be silly.' . . . I think that epitomizes for you something more than the Hlanzeni mission. You have most missions there in a nutshell: 'What is a virgin?' They simply don't know."

"O, God," said Friston. "But who's this man d'Elvadere?"

"That," I declared, "is a very big question. He looks like a Viking, and his manners are ducal. From a worldly point of view he is a failure, but I am inclined to think that he is a marvellous success. I almost suspect that he is one of those rare people who can do more with Africa than Africa can do with them. He's a gentleman, and quite a good blacksmith. He has no money and he used to drink. I call him a voluptuous pioneer. He reached Goldenville when it was nothing but a few tents. He knew everybody there in the early days, all the celebrities, all the Empire-builders who consoled themselves, as he will tell you himself, with black women and bottles of brandy. You must meet him. He lives on a farm belonging to a woman called Dunford, right away up in those hills to the left, beyond Bloodfield's. As he's practically immovable, our best plan would be to go up there and see him. I'll take you up by car one Sunday—he's more than worth the journey."

"I should be delighted," said Friston.

Finally we parted, first delivering up the key of the house to the caretaker. The house was transfigured in the sun. Friston and I went off down the hill, each by a different path, he to Hlanzeni and I to Ovuzane. My last sight of Friston showed him striding along lapped round by the waving fiery grass, white-hot.

* 5 *

During the following week the weather was bitterly cold. One morning I came to the shop door to find old Nordalsgaard getting off his horse just outside. He was wearing a small felt hat and his nose was red with cold. His was a tragic face, otherwise he would have looked like a comedian. Or like a clown, especially as this particular morning his body was enclosed in a monstrous riding-coat of dull blue cloth and antique pattern; as thick as cardboard; with many buttons; with triangular flaps to the pockets; adorned with braid and shoulder-capes. (Africa, I reflected, is full of curious European survivals.) As the old man stood on the ground I saw that the waist was cut extremely tight, and thence the coat hung in long straight lines to his feet.

125

"Aha," he exclaimed, extending a fat soft hand, "you covet my coat. It was for my father when he was a beau. I wear it now because I have no other."

"I think it's very elegant," I said. "But I hope it's not true that you are thinking of going home to Norway?"

"It is."

The old man nodded, his face gloomy.

"It is indeed. My successor has arrived—the Reverend Rupert Friston, an Englishman. He is sent by my brother, Bishop Nordalsgaard, president of the Anglo-Scandinavian Board of Missions. You have met Mr Friston, no?"

"Yes: but d'you think he'll be able to carry on your work?"

"Ah, I am assailed with doubt. He seems a young man used to having his own way. But his father is Bishop of Crotchester: he ought to do——"

"But you'll only be away for a time?" I asked, knowing that he was to go for ever.

"Ah, no. I am going. I am going." He nodded his old head, and suddenly brightened. "But do you know what I came for? I have a golden piece of news. I came first to tell you. Nobody else knows. You can guess, no?"

I was puzzled.

"I am engaged to be married to Miss Rosa Grundso," he announced.

I was genuinely glad. It pleased me to think that that kind old man and that honest old woman could find mutual tenderness in their old age. I congratulated him.

"Don't you think people will laugh at us——?" he asked apprehensively.

"Why should they? You've done a very wise thing. You'll have somebody to look after you now."

And within a few days I was over at Hlanzeni to his wedding, in a churchful of blacks. Friston took the service in English, wearing a black cassock and a Lutheran ruff. He was a little cynical. The natives thought him extremely handsome. They were excited with pleasure.

The wedding-breakfast was set out on a long table in the dining-room. There were a great many tinned fruits set out in silver dishes, together with sweet cakes and pastries. To drink there was only coffee. A babble of silly talk grew louder and louder, the excited stupidity of a roomful of brainless Scandinavians, Germans and Dutchmen, mostly half-Anglicized, assembled at short notice from remote missions and penniless farms, and from behind the counters of Aucampstroom. The best man had cruel Teutonic eyes, and his lemon-green-coloured boots, aggressively new, squeaked with an intensity that made itself heard even above the conversation.

Old Nordalsgaard, the cause of what I can only call this demonstration, was able to detach himself, and came to me in a corner with a dejected air, as though he were assisting at a funeral. It was his wedding-day. The stooping shoulders were more bent than ever, and the aged bridegroom held himself like one battered by storms and worn out by anxiety, in a frock-coat, black, and as long as a shroud. With a charming inconsequence he drew me away to the next room. It was nearly dark in there that sunny morning. There was only the poorest straggling light, dimmed by foliage and the deep verandah outside, and further dimmed by thick lace curtains hung across the windows. Indeed, so ill-lighted was the room that it gave only to the eye half-hidden planes and surfaces of highly polished wood at intervals in the gloom, varied with crude pieces of tapestry and embroidery gaunt with wool. So sombre was the room, that the eye, roving, could find only tactile sensations in the light dissembled—the smoothness of the wood and the roughness of the wool. I could detect the presence of dust and cobwebs, a secret accumulation of dirt, and the first odour of antiquity. It was surprising in Africa (or was it surprising?) to find oneself in a haunted room.

We were standing near the obscured window. The old missionary's head, too heavy, was close to mine. His nose and eyes were red from weeping, and those arching wrinkles, line over line, stood out white upon his forehead like swollen veins.

"I have been here more than forty years," he said simply.

He took hold of my left arm gently with his right hand.

"I look back. I wonder what I have accomplished?"

His old eyes had tears.

Ah, but you must know that I was utterly moved. I was shaken. I was suddenly filled with the madness of vision. What was it before me? The encroachment of Africa? Was it not the nineteenth century, slowly disintegrating? The eighteenth, the seventeenth century; the Middle Ages? This old man was time. He was more than time. He had set out once, how finely. He had been purposeful. O, he had gone out with gifts and weapons, this man. His blood had been tradition; his brain, knowledge; his body, purpose. He had gone out, this old man, this old-world man, with a deliberate, elegant, mincing step to conquer Africa, to conquer the world, to conquer time. It was not a wreck: you could not call it a failure, this. It was defeat.

So he had come to the wilderness then, and now he was weeping with childlike rage and fear; with the ineffectual, the disillusioned, the unnoticed, the helpless, the hopeless, the uncontrolled, the quiet and utterly abandoned despair of old age. What had he done? What had he done? He had wounded history. The high-bred gentleman had left for his monument Olaf Shaw, a middle-class half-caste, second-rate. And what else?

Nordalsgaard trembled, and drew in his breath miserably. It was his wedding-day. We went back. Of course they had not missed him in the other room. Friston had a society manner. Mrs Nordalsgaard was busy memorizing recipes dictated by a *hausfrau*. The guests were noisy. Several native teachers and parsons were standing aloof, on their dignity. Olaf Shaw was there. He had come for the occasion. He was silent. His collar was uncomfortable.

As the coffee was getting cold the bridegroom began to read telegrams and letters of congratulation. The company sat down and applauded. When Nordalsgaard had finished, they sang doleful hymns.

But above the droning could be heard, with a distinct and awful and unceasing significance, the loud roar of chaos. And there could be felt that which Couperus found in Java, weighing down on his senses, 'the hidden force'.

★ 6 ★

Within a week Nordalsgaard and his wife had departed. Natives came from far and near to say good-bye. Weeping there was, and an interminable making of speeches. The weather was very hot again, and after a wandering service in the church, lasting three hours, the old missionary continued his farewells under an immense indigenous tree in the church-yard.

There was present an old mad woman, a witch who entertained herself with a unique form of Christianity, as wild as herself, its professor. She took it upon herself to throw her arms round Nordalsgaard's ample waist, and with a wide and toothless grin she clung to him, grimacing, and rubbing her lousy old head on his coat all the while that he was shaking hands with an endless procession of natives: but occasionally he patted the old witch vaguely, and this was her happiness.

The old man stood in the chequered shade, hatless, holding his bent back straighter than usual, very white in the face. A coloured decoration in the form of a cross was pinned to his frock-coat: it was the Order of St Valborg. His forehead was more wrinkled than ever, and he continually nodded his head. He spoke few words, and there were no sounds but sobbing, the quiet inarticulate cackling of the witch, and the chinking of little presents of money, brought by every black. The sun was intensely hot. No movement in the air was perceptible to the people, but a grove of banana trees in the background was never still. The long flat leaves, tenderly green, varied with leaves more tenderly yellow, were moving, moving a little, a very little, vaguely, uneasily, all the time. Their movements were as sad as those of beautiful and unhappy women stirring in their sleep, and from them there came to the ears of the crowd, now and again, poignant and remote like the voice of a ghost, the slightest imaginable sighing. . . .

It was the last that Hlanzeni saw of Nordalsgaard. I shuddered, I don't know why, to think of Friston and the future.

★ 7 ★

I motored Friston up to Mrs Dunford's at Ovuzanyana to see d'Elvadere. His mountain of green glass beer-bottles was winking in the sun, and he himself was sharpening a chisel on an oilstone, standing in the open air.

"It's not often a parson comes over here," he declared. "The last one was a stinking dissenter, and asked me if I was saved. I sang him accordingly a little song we used to sing years ago:

> 'Safe in the arms of Jesus,
> Safe in Pretoria gaol—
> Fourteen days' hard labour
> For cutting off a donkey's tail. . . .'

'Don't blaspheme,' said the nasty minister when I had finished singing.

'Why not?' I said. 'Don't interfere with my immortal soul.'

'But it is my business,' he said.

'On the contrary,' I said, 'allow me to consider it mine.'

'You're very stubborn,' he said.

'I know,' I said. 'And you're very impertinent.'

'Let not your heart be hardened,' he said.

'No,' I said, 'I won't. And let not your head be softened.'

'Do you know who I am?' he said.

'No,' I said, 'and I don't want to know. But I know where you ought to be:

> 'Safe in the arms of Jesus
> Safe in Pretoria gaol—' "

D'Elvadere chuckled heartily, looking at Friston to see if he had shocked him.

"So this is Mr Friston," he said. "You don't *look* like a dissenter——"

"But he is," I said, "a kind of dissenter, a priest of the Lutheran-Catholic Church. He is the missionary who has taken the place of Nordalsgaard at Hlanzeni."

"Missionary!" shouted old Frank. "Don't talk to me about missionaries! Did I ever tell you about Tom Frickasea, the Bishop of Bathobazolo? Now, he *was* a missionary. First he was kicked out of the Church of Rome into the Church of England; then he was kicked out of that too. Then Tom started his own church. It was called The Church Militant. It was. Very militant. If anything got in Tom's way, they say, he used to blot it out. He was a steam-roller missionary. Tom Frickasea was the only parson in The Church Militant, and the only white. He called himself a bishop, and built himself a cathedral at Bathobazolo, one hundred and twenty miles from the nearest white man, in a God-forsaken and man-forsaken corner of Swedish East Africa. The cathedral was a fine building, but it had no windows. Don't ask me what went on inside. There was a lot of hanky-panky with candles and smells and images and vestments. But he had his niggers in wonderful control. They say The Church Militant ran like a machine. He made a hell of a lot of money out of that show: then he set fire to the cathedral and cleared out. He went home and married as well as you could wish: I saw the notice in *The Times*:

Thomas Charles Edward Ferdinand Sangroyal Frickasea, eldest son of Sir Thomas Frickasea, Bart., of Sangroyal Abbey, South-ants, and Lady Mary Philbrook, only daughter of the Earl and Countess of Shipcastle.

"Now, Friston, there's an example for you. Go thou, my son, and do likewise."

Friston was entertained.

"Parsons are the devil," continued old Frank, "but parsons' sons——! Of course that's an old story, but I know what I'm talking about—I'm a parson's son myself. O yes, I'm quite a good example. Those beer-bottles that you saw at the back are not mine, Mr Friston. That little collection was made by another parson's son, what they call a remittance-man. You haven't been very long in Africa, Mr Friston? Well, now you see the Empire-builder at home. I think he'd better give you some lunch. Bully beef and pickles. You've come to take Nordalsgaard's place, Mr Friston?"

"I have," said Friston. "What did you think of Nordalsgaard?"

"What do I think of any missionary? Nordalsgaard was a decent enough old man, but he hadn't the shadow of an idea of what he was playing at. I don't suppose you want advice, but if you want information you can get it from me."

"I'm all ears," said Friston.

"Well, you must remember that there are different kinds of missionaries. In this country they nearly all drink, and they nearly all keep black women: I don't know about other countries. There are, of course, a few conscientious fools; but they are very rare. There are don't-care-a-damns, who just muddle along. There are plenty of get-rich-quicklies; they're very wise. And there are what I call intellectual researchers—the rarest kind of missionary: they are people who won't generally believe a thing till they've proved it; people who really want to do good by the natives, but only when they're sure they're working on the right lines. Mr Friston is going to be an intellectual researcher."

He turned to me.

"And you would be an intellectual researcher, too," he said, "if you were a missionary. Now I'll give you an example of the conscientious fool. He's very rare. He's the Reverend Phineas Crow, American Baptist. He came out here with a wife and brat, but he said they got between him and his work, so he sent them back home. Out in the *veld* one day Mr Crow met a raw native, wearing nothing but a skin round his middle, and a few beads.

'Good-morning,' said the missionary, 'if you'll give me your clothes I'll give you mine.'

"The nigger thought he was mad, and tried to get away: but the Baptist battered him. It was a knock-out blow. Phineas Crow came home nearly nude, while the nigger lay gasping upon his back in linen underclothes, a dickey, a back-to-front celluloid collar, a black serge suit, black socks, black boots, gent's watch and albert, and black shovel hat. Crow took to living in a mud hut, and ended up with one convert, a half-witted black, a female."

"Now, Friston," continued old Frank, "let me tell you this. You needn't listen if you don't want to. Never suppose that you can elevate the black man to your own level. You can't. I wouldn't give two straws for all this rubbish about 'uplift'. But it is very easy for a white man to lower himself to the level of the native. And, for that very reason, do not allow yourself to believe that, because South Africa is painted red upon the map and has at present a white population of a million and a half, it is in consequence a white man's country. It is nothing of the sort. It can never be anything but a black, or at least a coloured man's country. Now, Mr Friston, get on with your intellectual research, and don't forget what old Frank told you."

134

"Tell me," said Friston, "your views about miscegenation."

"But my views are biased, Mr Friston. I cannot claim that no black woman has ever shared my bed——"

★ 8 ★

We had just finished lunch, and were preparing to smoke. D'Elvadere paused, a match in his hand.

"I can hear a horse," he said, and he got up and went out of the room. Friston and I were left alone a moment. The hut seemed transfigured with warmth and light reflected from the rocky walls outside. It was not long after mid-day. We had drunk nothing but the thinnest of beer, but all at once I was taken with a curious sensation of light-headedness. Friston, in the glow of heat, looked like a different person. Through the open door I gazed at a craggy hill-side. Dazzling rocks were scattered thick on the summer grass, and ascending among them, like tongues of fire, was a flock of sheep. One ran a little before the others, up: and another two came up. Up again climbed two more. One. One or two again. Two, up. The whole flock climbing with a gradual rhythm their ascent had the intensity of a dream. Golden fleeces, I thought. I heard an approach of voices, as from another life. Ah, this was Medea. But Jason——?

It was Mabel van der Horst standing in the doorway, the housekeeper at Mrs Dunford's.

With open meshes and a wide brim, a flat straw hat lay upon her head like an inverted basket, within which was held her darkish hair, whose lustre had the richness of fruit—her darkish vigorous hair, that was thatched softly and closely about her ears. Her skin was rosier than I had been given to notice among Colonial women, its radiance heightened by the radiance of the room and its summery warmth. She wore no ornament, and a white dress loose in the body, short in the skirt, and nearly sleeveless. There was in her hand a short branch of wattle, sprigged with pollenous flowers, that she had for a riding-switch. But she had a certain angularity of feature and a certain awkwardness of bearing. She had a brusque way of talking that I took for a token of a mind that it was worth supposing to be original. She had given me from the first to believe that she was a woman of character: it was a belief upon which subsequently I never had reason to go back.

Mabel and Friston got on together like a house on fire.

"I'm obstinate," I heard her declaring to him, "and I know I am. Even at school they could never make me believe things because I was told to believe them. They could never make me do things unless I myself had a very good reason for doing them. The headmistress once brought on me the monstrous accusation of being unladylike. It was the nastiest thing she could think of saying. 'Miss Springorum,' I said, 'I thank God on my bended knees that I am not a lady.'"

Old Frank laughed very heartily at this, his mouth wide open under his golden moustaches.

"Most of the girls," continued Miss van der Horst, "were simply feather-pated. They thought I was quite mad because I found more in life and got more out of life than they ever dreamt of. They thought I was mad, Mr Parson, just as I think you're mad if you really believe that the late Mr Christ was God. He was no more a god than you are."

Friston was alarmed.

"O, look here, let's keep off all that. I'm not going to talk shop to-day. Let's get on to politics instead. Now then, let's hear your views about the native question, for instance?"

"I like the way you change the subject when a lidy's talking. But poof!" the woman exclaimed, "native question! What the hell *is* the native question? You take away the black man's country, and, shirking the future consequences of your action, you blindly affix a label to what you know (and fear) the black man is thinking of you—'the native question'. Native question, indeed! My good man, there is no native question. It isn't a question. It's an answer. I don't know whether people are wilfully blind, that they can't see what's coming. The white man's as dead as a doornail in this country. You gain nothing by not looking facts in the face. All this Empire-building's a blooming blind alley. We think we're invincible because we can fly round the world in an aeroplane, and because we can send our silly voices flying round the world by wireless. Wait a little, the black man will break our aeroplanes, and the yellow man will effectually silence even our loudest loud-speakers. The strength of the natives is in their weakness."

"Friston," I said, "you and Miss van der Horst ought to agree."

"We do," he said.

"You both think," I said, "that the world is for dagoes. Neither of you has any faith in the white man's future, or in the white man himself."

"We haven't," said Friston.

"Why not?"

"Well, Europe is as dead as mutton. And where Europe isn't dead it is Satanist."

"Possibly," I said. "But America?"

"America? It's proved that one American in ten has negro blood."

"Yes," I said, "that's all very well, there may be intermixture going on: we know there is in this country, at any rate. But the psychologists say that there is in the white race an unconquerable aversion from colour. The exception, once again, proves the rule. I should like your reasons."

"My prophecies belong," said Friston, "as I myself belong, to the world of dreams, which is the actual world. The world we live in simply reflects part of the truth from that other, that actual world of dreams. In this I see no call for reason. It is not a rational matter, but an emotional. If you want reasons, I should say the dying-out of Christianity; the increase of mysticism and occultism and moral and sexual perversion; the ever quicker and quicker ways of getting about from place to place in the modern world, and the consequent annihilation of distance; the influences of various climates and environments upon ever-increasing numbers of people; and above all the slow birth of the individual. He is emerging with infinite travail from the womb of time. I tell you there's no call for reason. I don't use my eyes and ears so much as my nerves, so where does reason come in? The process of discovering truth I call 'understanding with the nerves'."

"I see Friston as an optimist," said the woman. "For him all's for the best in the best of all possible worlds. He sees his half-caste world coming, and he wants adequately to prepare the way. I think he believes that is more suitable work for a missionary than teaching the natives that Esau was a hairy man, or whatever it is they teach in Sunday-schools. His best plan at Hlanzeni would be to get together some sort of association for the furtherance of his aims. You see the idea?—a society of small size, great energy, and clear views, called, let us say, Young Africa. How it would stir the poor whites!"

"It's a very sound idea," said Friston slowly, "but of course you would have to be a member."

"I should be delighted," said Mabel van der Horst.

I turned to old Frank.

"I like the idea. As these two say, you can't go on for ever with Empire-building."

"But that's exactly what I said thirty years ago in Bladesia —only it wasn't called that then, it was called Tukulululand —when I saw the great invincible high and mighty Nigel Blades laid out by a bottle of brandy. There's been more tripe talked about that man than anybody else in creation. I said then, 'Is this all that Empire-building leads to?'

'O,' they said, 'you must forgive a little to a man that's done so much. Look at the Trans-African Railways. Look at the Dark Continent Exploration Company,' they said, 'what about that?'

'Well, what about it?' I said. 'I should call it the Dark Continent Exploitation Company. It's a blind alley. Can't you see that Blades is a murderer? He's helping to kill the white race.'

'You mean the brandy-bottle?' they said.

'No,' I told them, 'I mean the excuses you bring forward for the brandy-bottle.'

"They used to snigger because they couldn't understand. No doubt they would still snigger. But in a few years' time——"

D'Elvadere shrugged his shoulders very slightly, with distinction. It is an art that is not practised elegantly by Colonials.

When we went away the old man filled up his doorway.

He was smoking a pipe, and the westering sun lit him up with rose and gold, the pioneer, the iconoclast.

Mabel van der Horst was sitting in the saddle when Friston and I drove off in the car. She had a cigarette, and gave us good-bye with the intimate grace of an animal.

★ 9 ★

Of the political organization in which Friston's hopes (and perhaps Mabel van der Horst's and to some extent mine) had root, Young Africa, the first meeting was held at the Hlanzeni Mission, in that room which for me could be concerned only at any time or under any stress with Nordalsgaard, its gloom being his gloom, its air of anxiety and mournful expectation his. There was Friston, at the head of the table, eager and excited, very self-contained, with a patch of cherry-rose on either cheek-bone, his face as highly coloured as his hopes. At his right sat Zachary Msomi, slightly contemptuous, the kaffir intellectual, his over-developed torso constricted in a black coat. He had lately been ordained, and now occupied a position at Hlanzeni only second in importance to Friston's.

It had been agreed to invite him to join Young Africa by reason of his character, about which Friston thought he knew something. He was to act as secretary, and his long black hands were busy with pens, ink and paper.

I arrived rather late with Caleb, whom I had insisted on bringing, a person of great good sense. Mabel van der Horst took the end of the table opposite to Friston, sitting in a high chair and dominating us all.

"If he were here," Caleb said, "I wonder what Mr Nordalsgaard would say?"

"I shouldn't think it matters very much what he would say," said Mabel.

"Order," said the chairman.

We didn't get very far at that first meeting.

"We want to make up our minds about several things that concern us. The positions of religion and politics in native education, for instance, and miscegenation. I am here at Hlanzeni to do my best, and I can see already that the natives want something more than neo-Lutheranism."

"Hear, hear," said Zachary, in a deep voice.

There was a lot of ineffectual conversation. I remember phrases. Make up our minds. Silence for the time being. Official curiosity. Political propaganda. Next meeting at Silver Hill. Then Mabel suggested that we should ask d'Elvadere to join us.

"You'd never get him off the farm," I said.

"He's a charming old man," said Friston, "but he's lived so long among people a long way below him that he has been thrown out of joint, as it were. He has the keenest perceptions, but his sense of humour (for example) is very crude. I'm afraid he would be bitter and extreme. The faults of being bitter and extreme are supposed to be youthful faults, but I think you will agree with me that, although we fully appreciate Mr d'Elvadere's many good qualities, yet we recognize that there is no bitterness like old bitterness, and no extremist like an old extremist."

We all felt that Friston was right.

★ 10 ★

The second meeting of Young Africa was duly held at Silver Hill. We sat in the same order as before round a large bare table in the large bare room where I had first seen Friston. I thought of the Schwerdts, whose memory hung like an evil spirit over the place.

I had seen from their first meeting that Friston was more than a little taken with Mabel, while she seemed to have in her manner towards him no more than friendliness. But now a certain truth came upon me with the suddenness of a revelation. I did not seem so much to be seized with a mental realization of a plain fact as with a cold physical terror. I was intestinally sick, as at a catastrophe. It was clear that Mabel van der Horst was attracted, how slightly it was hard to measure, towards Zachary Msomi. It was one thing to talk glibly about miscegenation, to fool about with an idea, and another to find oneself face to face with the actual happening: it was the difference between a box of matches and a house on fire.

I found myself detached, and I knew myself powerless. I could foresee the birth of rivalry between those two men: the one black, the other white. I felt myself to be like a scientist who watches some enormity of nature through a microscope—I was an entomologist observing the titanic and elemental lusts of beetles infinitesimal in a tiny battleground, where blades of grass were greater than tree-trunks, and the dynamics of sex were rending hearts. I knew that the matter would proceed with the almost automatic cruelty peculiar to such occasions.

After the meeting I said to Mabel:

"You admire Zachary Msomi?"

"He's something more than the usual native," she said vaguely.

"I think you would regret it," I directly told her, "if you were to allow yourself to have too good an opinion of him."

"D'you think so?" she sneered. "My good Wolfe, mind your own business."

After that I let things take their course.

At the meeting we had discussed the basis of an article to be contributed by Caleb to *The Morning Star*, a leading native newspaper, that circulates throughout southern Africa. When the article appeared it turned out to be rather amusing. Here it is:

"YOUNG AFRICA"

AN IMPORTANT NEW MOVEMENT FOR THE REGENERATION OF OUR COUNTRY

By Caleb Msomi, Assistant Secretary

A sentiment of uneasiness and dissatisfaction with the existing state of affairs as they are has for some time manifested itself amongst the most advanced and enlightened of the European and Bantu Intelligentsia, and this circumstance has culminated in the formation of an organisation designed to promote accuracy of political and religious opinion and energy of furtherance of sociological positions and welfares of Bantu peoples and peoples throughout the Continent of Africa that is our Fatherland, and Elsewhere. This movement owes its inception to the good offices of the newly-instated missionary at the well-known Lutheran-Catholic mission-station at Hlanzeni, via Aucampstroom, formerly controlled by the Rev. Otto Nordals-

gaard, successor to the renowned late Bishop Klodquist, and now by the Rev. Rupert Friston, of whom it is we are speaking, who is assisted in his praiseworthy enterprise by Mr Turbott Wolfe of Ovuzane Trading Station, a well-known and some-time-established Lembuland-storekeeper, who are in turn assisted by a number of helping and well-wishing sympathizers, of whom the writer of this article considers himself fortunate to be counted one, acting as he is in his capacity as Assistant Secretary, as he writes this article herewith. It is extra-superfinely fortunate for the auspices of the Association and happily portends that its two leading members or founders should occur to be Europeans familiar with prevailing sociological conditions as they are amongst the native peoples. There is also the writer of this article understands an European lady associated in the executive of the organisation which is a happy Auspice.

To put it in a Nutshell, WE BELIEVE:

1. That Africa is not the white man's country.

2. That miscegenation is the only way for Africa to be secured to the Africans.

3. That it is inevitable, right and proper.

4. That if it can be shown to be so, we shall have laid true foundations for the future Coloured World.

5. That we are pioneers.

———

NOTE, Intending Members are asked to pay no Money, but must subscribe their names to the above beliefs and spread propaganda. All communications to be addressed to the Secretary or Assistant Secretary of Young Africa, Ovuzane M.S., via Aucampstroom, Lembuland.

That document—said Turbott Wolfe—shows you what

you're up against when you approach the native point of view with an air of discovery. Before it was printed Caleb had brought it humbly to me to be corrected. I should not recommend the style, but I had not the heart to alter a word: it would have done away at a blow with Caleb's illusion that he could talk and write English.

Friston was surprised that the article brought no word to us of official or ecclesiastical or even private rebuke.

"They're all asleep," I told him, "except the officials, who have seen the paper and are too cunning to speak. They're awaiting further developments before they come down on you like a ton of bricks. I think we ought to walk warily."

"Walk warily be blowed," he said. "We're going our own way."

3

ONLY a few days after that second meeting I had a bout
of illness. It began with influenza and it ended with
complications. I may have had a touch of the local fever. The
Aucampstroom doctor, more of a fool than most of his kind,
was unable to do me much good. He recommended a change
of air, and suggested that I should billet myself with some
people called Soper, at a farm that lay very high up in the
Ovuzanyana mountains, on the farther side of Aucampstroom. The Sopers' farm, he told me, was not very far from
Mrs Dunford's, but at a much greater altitude. I looked forward to the prospect of seeing something of Mabel van der
Horst and old Frank d'Elvadere, so it was with a pleasant
thrill (perhaps I can talk her out of her feeling for Zachary, I
said to myself) that I found myself seated beside Soper in a
tall and jolting Cape-cart one afternoon; that I found myself
snuffing the icy mountain air that blew straight down from
the heights into the harsh and dusty alleys of Aucampstroom.
Soper was a short wiry fierce ungainly excitable man with a
very red face; a man very heartily disliked because he worked
harder and achieved more than his neighbours. As soon as I
saw Soper I felt that however much I might find myself at
variance with him yet he was at any rate honest. His eyes
were of the same candid topaz-yellow as those of the sheep
that brought him a living: behind them you could almost
see his harsh narrow little brain tucked up in its harsh narrow
little bed. I was surprised to hear him saying:

"Old Frank d'Elvadere—d'you know him? He's staying with me for a few days. He has broken with old Mrs Dunford. I reckon myself he's treated the old lady very badly. Eleven years he's been there, and they've done everything for him, absolutely everything. Man, he went there without a penny, without even a single tool, and they've given him a good home, and he's had an easier time there than he'd ever be likely to get anywhere else. He's not a fool, he's a lunatic. What can he do at his age? I told him he could just come to us at Soper's End until he can get something to do. He's brought all his blooming tools with him too."

It was plain that the unfortunate d'Elvadere was an unwelcome guest.

"We've got a queer lot in these parts," Soper went on, "and old Frank's not the only one. Now I saw old Fotheringhay in town this morning. A fine minister he is. I should like to know what he thinks he does for a living. We never see him out our way from one year's end to another. He's practically kept going by Alfredson. You know Alfredson, in Aucampstroom?"

I knew Alfredson by sight, the leading tradesman.

"Well, there you are. Alfredson's coloured, do you know that? A touch of the tar-brush there, all right. You look at his nails. You can always tell them by their nails. Nails and eyes. You thought he was white? *White?* He's no more white than any blooming nigger on my farm. St Helena, or Jamaica, or Jerusalem or somewhere it was that Alfredson came from. Where are the West Indies again? Well, it was somewhere there that he came from. O yes, there's more than a touch of the tar-brush there, all right. Man, he's got a pretty daughter, Alfredson has. Pretty? Man, but she's a pretty girl. I don't fancy colour myself, but I'm ready to admit that I nearly married that girl before I met Mrs Soper. Well, Alfredson simply keeps those Fotheringhays. His word's law to them. They could never live on the stipend or dole or whatever it is these parsons get. What is the term again? Anyway, it's Alfredson that keeps them going. I don't understand old Fotheringhay. He seems to have a hell of an opinion of himself. They say the old lady's about ten years older than he is. He married her for her money, but she brought nothing with her, and when her father died there was nothing left, so they say. Old Fotheringhay had to make the best of a bad job. They seem to get along all right. But they're queer people. I never did like them myself. These ministers are all humbugs. All humbugs, they are. And you won't tell me they're not."

A generalization on the part of Soper hardly seemed to admit of contradiction, or even of modification. But it is not only a characteristic of the ignorant, I reflected, to lay down laws.

"Well," continued Soper, scarlet in the face, "when I saw old Fotheringhay this morning he told me you've got a new bloody missionary down at Hlanzeni. Ugh, these missionaries——! Only lately out from England. What's the brute's name again? A shocking memory for names I have. Man, d'you think I can ever remember a name?"

"His name's Friston," I said.

"Friston! Yes, that's it. Friston. I knew it began with an F. D'you know the chap at all?"

"I've just met him," I said.

"Fotheringhay tells me—in fact they're all talking about him. They say he's got a lot of tomfool ideas about the niggers. Love one another, you see, and all that sort of bloody nonsense. Native gentlemen—our black brothers! Man, it makes me sick, that kind of thing does. Hell, they're no better than animals. He'll learn his mistake pretty quick. What did you think of him when you saw him?"

"I thought he was a man of character," I said.

"O, I don't say he isn't. Bloody silly character, anyway. Yes, we've got enough fools round here already. The only man of the lot was old Max Dunford, and he's gone now. But these missionaries——"

I happened to know that Soper had been put on his feet financially by Mrs Dunford's late husband, at the very comfortable rate of twelve and one half per cent per annum.

"Yes; old Max," said Soper reminiscently. "He was a hard man in business, and he had no friends, but I always got on well with him. O yes, I got on well with old Max Dunford. Now the old lady's too eccentric for me, and I don't like that blooming Dutch governess or housekeeper or whatever it is she's got hold of there. A girl that wants putting in her place (that's the kitchen, I always reckon) and keeping there. There's a daughter Thelma, away at school, a fine girl—like her father—and there's an idiot son, a raving bloody idiot, but he's locked up."

The horses were slow, and Soper shook the reins impatiently. I noticed a deep scar on his wrist, and asked him how he got it.

"O, that! That's a long story. That might have landed me in gaol, that might. Look here, promise not to say a word of this out, and I'll tell you. One night, just after I married Mrs Soper, a young Dutchman, Romaine, came down and started knocking on our front door. It was about half-past ten. He's a near neighbour of ours, Romaine. I couldn't think what was up. Mrs Soper wasn't half scared. It was a hot summer's night, with thunder in the air, and *dark*. Man, it was dark that night. Well, these Dutch people had a young governess with them for this chap's brother and little sisters. She was living in an outside room, because the house was full. It's not a big house. Well, it was such a hot night she couldn't sleep, and she came to the door in her nightdress to get some air. Now there was a nigger, Jacop, that used to work as a waggon-driver for old Romaine. This particular night he was on his way home from a beer-drink. He saw the girl standing at the door. Well, you can guess what happened. Young Romaine used to go round last thing at night with a lantern to see if everything was all right. It was lambing-time, and that night he was out later than usual. He heard the nigger's voice in the outside room, and looked in——. Well, he didn't make a great fuss. He sent the girl to the house. Romaine's a hefty fellow. He tied the nigger down to the bed. Then, without disturbing a soul, he caught his horse in the paddock, dark as it was, and without troubling about a saddle came riding down to me, hell-for-leather. Man, d'you know what we did? We castrated that nigger. We did. It was what he deserved, and he got it. The storm came. I've never seen such thunder and lightning in all my life. We kicked the nigger out. Man, talk about rain! I've never seen such rain as there was that night. We spent the night in that room. Romaine woke me up at about three in the morning.

'*Magtig!*' he said, 'supposing Jacop dies——'

'Supposing he does?' I said.

'Well,' he said, 'that's murder.'

'Get away,' I said, 'it's justifiable homicide.'

Romaine was in an awful state. As soon as it was anything like light he went out to look for Jacop. He didn't find him. But he found tracks that showed that the nigger had stepped over a *krantz* not far from the house, whether on purpose or not we never knew, in the dark rainy night. It was just as well for us. No trace was ever found of Jacop's body. Perhaps the jackals got it. Before I left for home in the morning, a policeman rode up to the door, soon after sunrise. Romaine got the fright of his life. He was shaking in his shoes. He thought he was in for the high jump.

'What's up, Romaine?' the policeman asked.

'Man,' he had the sense to say, 'I'm worried about our waggon-driver, Jacop. He went off to a beer-drink yesterday, and he's never come back. He's run off somewhere.'

'Is that all? Don't you worry about it, boy. He's only a —— nigger. He'll turn up.'

When I got home, Mrs Soper said to me:

'Ted, wherever have you been?'

'O,' I said, 'Romaine had some trouble with one of his best ewes last night. She was lambing, and he wanted me to give him a hand. We were rather a long time, so I thought I'd stay the night, especially as it was raining so hard.'

'He's an unusual kind of Dutchman,' Mrs Soper said. 'They don't often look after their stock like that.'

I could see Mrs Soper didn't believe a word I said. Wait, that's not all. After a time the girl was going to have a child, and the old Romaines kicked her out. She went to Aucampstroom. After the child was born she sent for Romaine and me to come together and see her. She said she wanted to tell us that Jacop had gone past her door that dark night. She had called him back. She it was, she said, who was to blame. She had asked him to come in. She loved him——

'Where is he now?' she asked.

'How do we know?' we said. 'He just cleared off.'

'Perhaps,' she said, with a knowing smile. She was nursing her little half-caste child. 'And perhaps not.'

I think she knew we had killed him. But these Dutch girls, you know—— Colour's nothing to them,"

"But the scar——" I said vaguely, hardly able to put my tongue to a word after such a history, "the scar on your wrist."

"That is where the nigger bit me."

★ 2 ★

The cart lurched into a broad untidy road littered with dust and rubbish, the approach to Soper's home. The farm buildings were clustered together between a grove of monumental evergreens and a jutting rocky hill like a promontory. The gloomy magnificent trees, twisted by fierce winds as by the nervous mental eye of a Van Gogh, had been planted only fifty years before by Soper's father. In their shadow now stood new barns and sheds, four-square, with shining iron roofs, that had been built by Soper himself. Beyond them was the house, almost untouched since it had been set up in the 'forties by some hardy *voortrekker*, a splendid and forgotten Dutch pioneer. He had called the farm Morgenzon, scratching its bitter acres for his bread in the intervals of Kaffir wars, his heart fed with an indomitable hope and purpose from a hidden source that is known only to pioneers.

Soper, gaunt and violent when he was not vulgar, seemed a worthy successor to this strong square house of stone, thickly thatched, in its small rank tree-ridden hedged-in garden, set between the harsh volcanic hill and a broad dam of water. The water flickered elusively with quivering lights and colours caught from the splendour of three titanic Lombardy poplars, and from the foliage, haunted with birds, of an African willow, serene, autumnal, mountainous.

Soper's wife came out to meet us, a large plain putty-coloured woman with no eyebrows, but not without a certain fineness in her almost Jewish features. She was fair in the hair and dark in the eyes, a type you find in the North of England. Soper's child was playing on a dungheap with a little native boy, his small mean soul getting coloured with the monstrous intangible darkness of the native point of view. The child was in danger. His birthright was being sold over his head.

Over Mrs Soper's shoulder I caught sight of a rocking-chair on the narrow verandah of the house. A sensitive chair; for the slightest of winds was rocking it backwards and forwards irregularly. It moved as one moves in the throes of a tearless grief, the arms hugged to the body, the hands covering the face. Unfortunate chair; what was moving it so? It was not this slightest of winds. No, it must be one of those stranger winds that rise and lapse in the imagination, stirring with the slightest uneasy wings *something* that cannot reveal itself, something supernatural.

It was cold, and we all went in—the wild man, his dense wife, the paying guest: but not the abandoned child.

"Come in, Sidnee, it's getting cold."

"Ow, mommee, can't I stay out a little? I like being out in the dark," the child whined. "Can't I stay out in the dark?"

"Yes; jest a few minutes, then. Mind when I call you, you must come in, and tell Ndebakabani to run along home."

Away in the dusk ran the jubilant white child and the black child, and we others went in to firelight and coffee. I wondered what had happened to old d'Elvadere.

"O, he's just sharing an out-house with a Dutch carpenter

who's here doing a job for me," said Soper. They did not appear.

Perhaps they were discussing Soper more quietly than he continued, in a harsh excitable voice, to discuss them, with more truth, I fear, than charity. I did not see old Frank until the following morning, and then only for a few minutes. He was laboriously building a cart in return for his keep.

Soper took me out partridge-shooting on the bleak uplands all the morning, and we came home tired and hungry to lunch. Only then did it become at all possible to discover how these various people stood in their personal relations to one another.

No sooner were we seated than I was able to realize how great a strain had been imposed on the meal just by virtue of the antagonisms of those who sat down to it.

D'Elvadere's dislike for the hollow gentility of these Colonials, his hatred of shams, was carefully bottled up. There was a feeling in the air that this old man was a distinguished guest, a noble stranger; an ornament to the table rather than an outcast on sufferance. The rigidity of the conversation had in it something of the same courtesy that might be found at a meeting in ancient days of several generals from opposing armies on the eve of a mighty battle. For some time there was no remark that stuck for five seconds in the head, and the talk fell from the weather and the crops to the very food upon the table. When meal-time talk turns to food, the food turns to fodder. Food should be discussed before meals, at meal-time eaten, and afterwards digested. But am I allowed to intrude my own opinions upon the narrative?

I can't recollect what sudden fatal turn of words it was that shaped the name of Max Dunford, but d'Elvadere found at once a chance to talk. Out of politeness he strove to be entertaining, but gallantry was quicker than discretion, rusted by years of silence. He began talking of the deceased Dunford's curious stammer.

"You know," he said, "it's always a great joke with the Kaffirs. In fact they used to call him Paddafanger, from that odd clucking noise he made when he was trying to get a word out. There was one chap over there at Rooirandtjes that used to take him off splendidly. I don't know if you remember him, a waggon-boy called Simon? Anyway, he was there for years. But he got the sack for giving old Max a thrashing. What happened was this. Old Max wanted to beat Simon for something he had done wrong, so he got hold of him and dragged him into the stable—that one with the heavy sliding doors that old Max built himself. He wanted to get Simon in there so that he could shut the doors, and then go for him with a big *sjambok* that was kept hanging up inside. He got Simon in all right; and shut the doors; and managed to get hold of the *sjambok*; but the funny thing was that when old Max tried to grab Simon it was Simon that grabbed old Max!"

Old Frank lay back in his chair with a broad delightful grin at the primitive irony of such a situation. (I remembered that Friston had called his sense of humour crude: Friston was right.) An ominous silence was only broken by some futile unnoticed comment of mine, and d'Elvadere plunged forward with the story.

"I think that day old Max got the biggest hiding he ever had in his life, and I daresay he deserved it. That nigger didn't half let into him—I suppose he felt he was undoing all his old smothered wrongs. Revenge is sweet. But all the time old Max was protesting, and spluttering and stuttering in Dutch and English and Lembu, and coughing up alternate threats and promises like a coward. When Simon had quite finished with him, he slipped out and shut those great doors on the outside, and waited till he heard old Max stammering to be let out."

Frank chuckled.

"Afterwards, on occasion, Simon used to come down to my hut. I have never heard anything better in my life than the way he imitated old Max Dunford trying to ask him to let go, between strokes of the whip. Simon wouldn't often do it, but sometimes, when I wanted a good laugh, I was able to get him going. You can just imagine it!"

D'Elvadere went on chuckling till two droll tears started out of his ageing eyes. He went on rocking with laughter, and then ponderously wiped his enormous moustaches with his dinner-napkin, looking round over the top for applause.

Dead silence.

I tried to come to the rescue. I sniggered. I said, for the sake of something to say:

"It must be pretty hard to imitate a man like that really well."

To prolong the fatuity of my remark I sniggered again.

Then I caught sight of Soper's face. It was positively drawn with rage. I remembered what poor old Frank evidently didn't consider, though he must have known. Max Dunford had been Soper's only friend, and the whole fabric of Soper's present existence had been constructed on a basis of money lent to him by Dunford.

I looked at Soper's yellow lascivious eyes, fixed on d'Elvadere, and heard him say bitterly, leaning across me:

"Do you really think that's funny, Frank?"

D'Elvadere was horribly taken unawares, but he didn't show it.

"What's funny?" he asked. "You mean the story? I think it's extremely funny: don't you?"

"Do you know what I think?" Soper shouted, in a flush. "Do you know what I think? I think a man who can get a blasted Kaffir to make fun of another white man ought to be ashamed of himself. Man, where on earth should we all be if people started running us down to our own niggers? You Home-born chaps! You never seem to know——"

"It's hardly a question of being Home-born," d'Elvadere interrupted in a very quiet voice. "I lived twenty-five years in this God-forsaken country before you were born. Good Lord! I'm old enough to be your grandfather. You needn't lecture me."

"I'm damn well going to lecture you! It's disgusting. You had no business—no right—no right at all—to get hold of one of Max Dunford's own niggers like that and encourage him to run Max Dunford down. I never thought you were the sort of chap to go and do a dirty thing like that. You ought to be ashamed of yourself. Man, you ought to be ashamed of yourself!"

Soper was leaning forward, scarlet in the face.

"D'you mean to tell me it's right?" he screamed.

D'Elvadere pushed away his plate, adorned with the ruins of cold mutton and warm grease, and again wiped his golden moustaches, this time very deliberately. He began to stare languidly before him with a greater air of detachment than a deaf-mute. Soper's question left him cold.

"D'you think it's right, Frank? I'm asking you!"

D'Elvadere turned very slowly from the waist and looked at Soper for a moment with the utmost weariness, and then he turned very slowly to his former position. Without a word. A deadly silence. His patriarchal arms were resting on the arms of the chair.

Mrs Soper was wearing a dollish look of impudent scorn, holding her silly mental nose (as it were) between uncared-for mental fingers. This was the best she could do in support of her husband. If she had been a woman worth her salt she could have saved the situation with a gesture.

The Dutch carpenter, on the other side of the table, was gaping like a codfish. He recovered in so far as to be able to say:

"Not another speck, thanks, Mr Soper. No, I've done very well. Very tasty it was, that mutton. Very tasty, thanks."

And the gape fastened itself anew upon his fishy face.

Soper's wife at the end of the table was filling some enormous cups with lukewarm coffee.

I said:

"There are some insurance agents on the warpath. I suppose they will be here to-day or to-morrow."

"O, I've got no time for them," Soper exclaimed, trying with new violence to obscure his former violence. "Man, I've got no time for them. I always tell them I am insured, and when they ask me the name of the company I tell them to mind their own business. That's the way I deal with them. Man, insurance agents and Dutchmen I've got no time for. I always say that when you look at a Dutchman you look at a thief and a liar."

"That's a little sweeping," I remarked, with my eye on the unfortunate carpenter.

"Man, you don't know them as I know them. Look at my nearest neighbour over here—old Romaine. He doesn't even know the meaning of the word 'progress', and his sons are just like him. Only this morning I had to chase two scabby sheep of his out of my lands, and I caught my foot in a hole and nearly broke my ankle. I am certain he drives them in on purpose. If I've chased them once I've chased them a dozen times. I said to my old herd-boy before dinner, I said:

'*Magtig Jan! jy moet maar daardie skape slag. Oubaas Romaine maak my baie kwaad met sy verdomde skape. As jy dit nie doen nie, sal ek hulle self darem dood maak.*'"[1]

Soper leant back in his chair, red with triumph. He had only ordered one of his own native servants to destroy another white man's property. I would not, accordingly, have given at that moment so much as a penny for d'Elvadere's thoughts. There are times when human inconsistency passes the bounds of human belief.

Even when the meal was over old Frank d'Elvadere was sitting stock-still. He looked more like a waxwork than anything else. Soper's wife said "Excuse me" with a sniff, and went off into the kitchen, and I wandered out of doors with the carpenter. We left Soper and old Frank together.

"Well," said the carpenter, when we were hardly out of the house, "they say in Aucampstroom that Soper has no friends now, and only had one before. It was a pity that old Frank should pick upon the very man. I've seen some queer *kerels* in these parts, but Soper——! It's his eyes that I'm afraid of. Did you see his eyes? Man, I'm afraid of them. Mind you, I know what I'm talking about—I once went through the asylum at Valkenberg, and I know what a lunatic's eyes look like. Soper'll find himself in Valkenberg before he's done. Man, he's mad. I tell you, I'm afraid of his eyes."

---

[1] '*Good Lord, Jan! you'll have to slaughter those sheep. Old master Romaine drives me wild with his blasted sheep. If you're not going to do it, I'll have to kill them myself.*'

"Soper," I said, "has yellow eyes like a sheep's, and his face is getting long-boned like a sheep's face. He thinks of everything, I believe, in terms of sheep—except the deified Max Dunford."

"You're right there," said the carpenter. "If he could shear some wool off his wife he'd love her better. He would sell his grandmother to buy a fat *hamel.*"

He rubbed his hands and went off to his work. It was bitterly cold. It was just beginning to snow. This was an Africa, I reflected, quite different from Ovuzane. Here I was in another world. Snow, which I had only seen from Ovuzane on distant mountain-tops, now began to twirl out of a blind sky to my very feet. It was cold. I turned into the workshop where old Frank had been completing his cart and kindled the forge for warmth, awaiting his return. Twenty minutes afterwards he darkened the door, towering in with his pipe and his rosy face.

He said nothing for a few minutes more, but winked, and heaved an elephantine sigh. He knew that the violent Soper's heart was as cold as a stone. Frank's colossal shoulders were dismissing Soper, were dismissing all that Soper stood for and thrived on, with one slight shrug.

"He has pretty manners," I said. "I suppose he apologized?"

"O yes," said Frank, "he said he was sorry right enough; but what's the good of that? In any case I don't want to stay longer. I don't want to trespass on his precious hospitality. I've told him I'm going off to-morrow."

"Going off, Frank? Where on earth can you go?"

"I've got no more idea than you about that, but I have got an old moke of a horse, and I'm used to wandering about. I shall clear out of this district. To-morrow is Sunday, a very good day for travelling."

I was astounded at the calm way in which the old man proposed to *trek*. He might have been doing it weekly. He had been rooted solidly at Mrs Dunford's for eleven years. I didn't try and stop him from leaving Soper's. I think I would have done the same myself.

I can't forget old Frank that afternoon. He worked like a demigod. He had made up his mind to finish his job before he left. I don't suppose he wanted to feel afterwards in any way beholden to Soper. I lay on some sacks in a corner of the dark workshop and watched the old man musingly all the afternoon. A native was working the forge, and from it arose a continuous fountain of sparks before the brooding titan, who stood like an image, his eyes reflecting the fire they watched, his face running with sweat, his rosy cheeks and golden whiskers glowing. Every now and then he would urge on the sweating native, whose long bare curved back was bowed over the handle that worked the bellows, his elbows rising and falling, rising and falling, in a ceaseless rhythm. From time to time d'Elvadere would move across to the anvil that stood before a small square window, the only one that lighted the place, and the native would hold a red-hot piece of iron in the long blacksmith's-tongs while the old man smote it with a hammer, bending it, moulding it, piercing it; making the anvil cry 'cling-cling' at every touch like a mocking mechanical voice, like a bell.

I had a fancy that it was not Soper's iron he was striking, but Soper's mind. He was banging it with the incontrovertible force of his own character. A false analogy: Soper was a stone.

Only once did the man pause a moment from his work. The hammer in his hand rested upon the anvil. He had turned his head, and was looking out of the window. His face was lit by the snow outside with a bright bluish light. He was smiling profoundly.

That night was frosty, and the sun on the following morning scattered as soon as it appeared the surface of the snow with powdered diamonds. The sky assumed a luminous milky blue; and a few clouds were spread very far away, very far apart, by quiet unimaginable winds:

"... *and ye with starchy waves stiffen the liquid sky* ..."

You remember the line?

By eleven o'clock the snow had been thawed so rapidly by the African sun that only a few patches lay about the soaking yellow sward, and in the rocky hollows of the foothills. The jagged mountains were snow-white still, but the farm road was muddy, and the *vleis* were loud with living waters.

I walked down with d'Elvadere to Soper's boundary-gate, a couple of miles from the house. There we stood. The old man had his horse's reins looped over his arm.

"There are two things," he said. "that I always carry with me when I travel. One is this signet. It was given to me by my father. It once belonged to Mary, Queen of Scots. And there's this knife. I made it myself. The handle is made of some wood that was part of an old chair used by a famous Duchess of Floodwater in the Middle Ages. She was called Black Agnes. There is a story that she was once besieged in her castle, and found herself in a tight corner. The man who was besieging her sent two messengers with a proposal to raise the siege if she would consent to marry him. If she agreed she was to cause a flag to be hung over the battlements. She did not agree, so she had the two messengers hung out instead. When the invader broke into the castle Black

Agnes threw herself off the top rather than submit to her enemy's embraces. She was a fine woman——"

D'Elvadere seemed to me mediaeval just as Nordalsgaard had seemed mediaeval. Crude, but subtle.

He held out his hand.

"The very best of luck. God bless you, my son," said the man who had had no son. I was moved.

He climbed wearily into the saddle, and turned the horse's head. When he had gone some way he looked back over his shoulder, and nodded. The horse was a poor thing, and ambled down the long sloping road, ambled slowly, with that enormous old man upon its back, his long legs reaching nearly to the ground. His ponderous form was swaying slightly, slightly, and very evenly to the gentle motion of the horse. A light air came from somewhere and stirred the horse's tail, blowing it for a moment a little to the left. The sun was warm. The sky was a tender blue, more tender because of the sharp snow-white peaks, not very high, so near at hand. The old man did not turn his head again, and I was left with the sound of water, the emptying sound of water, running loudly in the ditches.

It was the last I saw of the voluptuous pioneer.

On my way back through the farm buildings I caught sight of the completed cart standing by itself in an open space: it was built like a dreadnought.

It was time for lunch.

"Are you ready for dinner?" Soper asked. He asked in such a way that I knew he meant 'Where have you been?'

As we sat down I remarked that I had been seeing off old Frank.

"O, I don't think he was worth it," was Soper's comment, "after the way he behaved yesterday. I should say 'misbehaved'. These old men get a bit soft in the head, living alone. They forget themselves."

"Do they?"

"But a man like old Frank ought to know better."

"Ought he?"

"Well, you know he ought," said Soper, in a pet.

I said:

"Perhaps you're right," in the tone of 'I think you're wrong.'

I couldn't help adding:

"But I'm afraid he has my sympathy."

Soper's expression when I said that was marvellous. He looked as though he doubted my sanity. I expected another outburst. His eyes bulged, and he said fiercely:

"Well, he's not worth arguing about, anyway."

Late in the afternoon I could see Soper through a window. There were two ploughs being drawn by teams of oxen round and round a small field near the house: Soper was following them, sowing broadcast. There was a harrow following him, to cover the seed. I could hear the natives calling out ceaselessly to the oxen. They were cracking their whips with a distinguished air. They went gracefully over the rough ground with their noble well-matched oxen, but Soper was stamping up and down: I could see his awkward bow-legs. He was thrusting his hand into a bag at his side, and throwing the seed angrily left, right: left, right. I saw it rise away from his hand in fountainous jets and fans as he went—left, right: left, right. Overhead, there were very distant clouds, smooth and placid in a milky sky. The shadows grew longer. The ploughs continued to turn over slick deep layers of wet red earth, redder than ever in the last sunlight when the rocky hills, obscured, were taking on a chill violet with the cold.

But Soper was still stamping up and down in his beautiful sodden field.

* 3 *

When I got back to Ovuzane—said Turbott Wolfe—it seemed that I was in another world. The air was warm, the country was fruitful. I could see no snow left even on the most distant summits of Ovuzanyana. But I felt suddenly, wretchedly sick when I thought that I had never once seen Mabel while I was staying with Soper. I felt that something frightful might have happened in my absence. I might be returning to a desolation. Mabel and Zachary, and Friston. I felt sure that Mabel's determination would be Friston's undoing. He is dreamy, I said, unbalanced. Dangerous. He admits it. Then this idea of miscegenation. How can I believe in it? It is a nightmare. This girl could not really mean to give herself to an African. She would be cutting herself clean off from her own world.

I did not gather from Caleb that he had heard or suspected anything in my absence.

"I am afraid of this miscegenation," he said. "I wonder if it is right. I ask myself——"

The very next day after my return I went over to Hlanzeni to find Friston.

The mission-house seemed so peaceful as I drove up in the car that I could hardly get myself to believe that it might become the scene of such horrors as I had imagined, with a sudden sickness; but conflagrations spring raging from a match.

I walked towards the house down a long alley arched over with gloomy indigenous trees, growing irregularly, older than the mission, forbidding roofs to a twilight made darker by the intense bright outer sunlight of the afternoon. The windows of the house were fitted with shutters, and these, painted black, lay flat against the sand-coloured walls. They seemed like pairs of hands with the palms turned outwards; they seemed to offer a polite denial of devilishness—but what was I thinking of?

The front door did not face the approach, but masked with a prolific vine, full of young leaves, hid itself in a garden of palms and flowering trees, planted in the days of the Great White Queen by the indefatigable Bishop Klodquist.

At the corner of the house there stood a water-butt. A flake of light had fled through the intricate roof of foliage above, and was dancing gently on the greenish water. It threw upon the wall, a few inches above the surface, a flickering light.

I looked back over my shoulder. The car stood waiting where I had left it, with that air of anxiety that a stationary vehicle always seems to wear on important occasions.

Important occasions, did I say? O God, yes: it was an important occasion. I went up the steps and knocked at the door. I thought I heard whispering within. I may have imagined it. I was admitted by Zachary, in a frock-coat. He seemed confused, or taken aback.

"You weren't expecting me?" I asked.

"O, Mr Wolfe, I am so glad you have come back. I am so glad you have come back. Mr Friston is possessed with a devil."

There was anxiety in his manner, and malice in his eyes.

I said:

"What on earth do you mean?"

For answer he pointed along a passage with a door at the end.

"That is his room. It will be best for you to go and see him yourself."

I paused on the threshold, hearing Friston's voice. He was laughing shrilly.

"Ha, ha!" I heard him screaming on the other side of the door. "Mr Friston indeed! You call yourself Friston? Let me introduce you to the other Mr Friston. Ha, ha, ha!"

This was intolerable. I opened the door.

Friston was dancing on his bed, stark naked. His two hands were clasped before him at arm's length, and he agitated them violently up and down.

"Mr Friston," he said in a low earnest voice, seeming not to notice my arrival, "this is Mr Friston."

He caught sight of me, standing with my back to the door, and his voice rose again.

"O, here's Wolfe! I needn't introduce you to Mr Friston, Wolfe. You know him already. Yes, Mr Friston, Wolfe knows the other Mr Friston quite well already. Wolfe thinks he knows him quite well——"

"Friston," I said, thoroughly irritated, "if you don't put your clothes on you'll catch cold, you fool."

"Fool, you say? Cold? What d'you think I took them off for? Mr Friston, Wolfe thinks you're a fool. Don't forget the 'mister'. *Mr* Wolfe thinks you're a fool. Tell him he's a fool himself. It's as hot as hell. Tell him that's why you took your clothes off——"

I made up my mind that Friston had been drinking, and decided to slip out and lock the door after me.

He saw me move.

"O, no, you don't! Tell Mr Wolfe to stay here, Mr Friston.

Tell him he's a ——! Mr Wolfe, just you stay here."

He leapt off the bed to detain me. I decided to humour him, as one would a lunatic.

"It's all right, Friston," I said. "I'm not going. I'm looking for a place to sit down."

"*Friston?* Who's Friston? Which Friston are you talking to? *Mr* Friston, you mean. And which Mr Friston, I ask you? because I want to know. Do you mean the Reverend Rupert Friston, who wears out his knees in ineffectual prayer? Or do you mean Friston that is possessed with a devil?"

I could hardly believe my ears.

"You see, Mr Wolfe, he does admit it himself," said the voice of Zachary, who was listening at the other side of the door. Friston became further maddened at the sound. He thrust me aside, and put his leering face to the keyhole.

"O, you black swine! Black, black, black; but my heart is blacker. I am a Satanist. Look out for Friston the Satanist! Look out for Satan himself! By God, or Baal, or Moloch, you listener-at-keyholes, if he gets hold of you, if I get hold of you, I'll bite your brains out. Oho, Young Africa, indeed!"

Friston staggered away from the door, and started laughing hideously. He slapped his thighs.

"Young Africa! Aha, ha, ha! You fools, you think you can deceive me. Let me tell you

> *Fear has withered swiftly since*
> HORROR *was written on the sun*——"

He clutched at a table.

"As for you, Wolfe, you ought to be called Sheep. You don't believe one thing you think. I don't believe one word you say. O, you slimy coward! Your god's Fear. So is mine. But wait till you see 'HORROR', my child, written on the sun.

Written, I tell you, in Roman capitals, right across the flaming sun. O, you coward! You take the cork out of the bottle, you twopenny fisherman, and out comes the genie. Or did I do it myself? Anyway, he won't go back. O no, don't you believe it! Not he. Pandora's box, you fool. D'you think the Devil's blind? Not he, not he!"

There was no doubt that he was out of his mind. I kept on reminding myself that lunatics must be humoured. But this was a raving lunatic——

"No," I said gently, "the Devil's not blind. But even the Devil must try and rest sometimes. Why don't you get into bed for a time?"

Friston fixed his unfortunate eyes upon me. They widened. His lips moved. There was no sound. He clutched for an instant at the air, and then fell headlong to the ground.

Zachary rushed in.

I knelt down to see if Friston was hurt. He seemed to have fallen so heavily. His shoulders quivered. Then his whole body was drawn and twisted in one dry gigantic sob.

He lay very still. His eyes were glazed, and his skin was chill, as the skin of a corpse is chill. I thought for a moment that he was dead. We lifted him into bed. He seemed very heavy. His chest heaved suddenly, and he sighed profoundly. His eyes closed. He was breathing evenly. He was in a deep sleep.

I went quietly to the window. The garden was gilded with the afternoon sun. There was an immense oleander just outside, weighed down with round pink flowers. Their slightly maddening scent invaded the room. The small blade-like leaves shivered in the windless air. I drew down the blind.

We went out of the room and locked the door. Outside, Zachary said:

"I am so glad you have come. It is s——."

You will know that word, my dear William Plomer—
said Turbott Wolfe—because you have been in Africa. You
know that s—— is a worse drug than hashish, the food of
assassins. The natives are addicted to it all over South Africa,
especially in Lembuland. There are different ways of preparing it. In Lembuland they mix it with the flowers of a herb
called m——. It is the wickedest of drugs, this mixture, one
of the most precious formulas of African witchcraft. How on
earth could Friston have got hold of it, I wondered? And,
having got hold of it, how could he have brought himself to
use it?

I followed Zachary into the dark room where I had been
with Nordalsgaard on his wedding-day. One of the doors
was open. At the end of the long adjoining room (once the
scene of the wedding-breakfast) another door was open. It
seemed to be that of a bedroom. How light it looked, suffused
with the quiet late sunlight. I could see the bed. There was a
woman's hat on the bed. It was the hat of Mabel van der
Horst.

★ 4 ★

"There is a draught in this room," said Zachary Msomi.
"Shall I shut the door?"

He shut the door slowly. He did not know what I had seen.
He said:

"I am concerned about the missionary. I believe he must
have been using s—— for about three days. I didn't think of
it before, but I see now. I have been trying to speak and reas-

on with him at meal-times, but he has been too stupid to answer, with bloodshot eyes of glass; or he has been coughing and dribbling; or raving, as you have seen him, like a madman; or asleep like an animal, as he is now. It has been hard to keep him from the sight of the people, especially the house-servants. I have said that he is ill, but they are beginning to doubt. I do not want them to think that their priest is no better than a common heathen."

I nodded. I felt myself filled with an overwhelming desire to get Friston away. It was plain that the relations between Zachary and Mabel were bringing about his sudden ruin.

I asked vaguely what could have made Friston smoke s——.

"Why do people take to drink?" said Zachary.

"The best plan would be for me to take him back with me now to Ovuzane," I suggested. "He would get a chance there to recover."

"You will never get him away," said Zachary hurriedly, "and even if you do, he will kill you. I tell you, Mr Wolfe, he is wild."

He did his best to dissuade me.

"As soon as it is dark," I ordered, "you will help me to carry him to the car. As soon as he is well I shall bring him back here. It is no use arguing. If you do, I shall take him to the public hospital at Aucampstroom. If he gets delirious there he might say anything. It is better that he should be with me. It doesn't matter what I hear."

Very soon after the sun was down we went together to Friston's room. We opened the door. It was quite dark. He was still breathing evenly, fast asleep. We wrapped him in a rug and carried him out to the car. He did not wake at all.

I got into the front seat, and before I started the engine

took Zachary's hand to say good-night. It was only then that Friston, on the back seat, began to stir. He mumbled in his sleep.

"Oho," he chuckled, "Africa for the Eurafricans!"

Zachary started violently, and quickly withdrew his hand.

"Good-night, Mr Wolfe; I can come if you want me."

I had never driven before so fast as I drove that night. When the headlights loomed upon the long white walls of home at Ovuzane I felt suddenly afraid.

Caleb was opening the garage doors. He asked no questions, and said no word but to greet me.

We carried Friston into the house, and laid him on a bed in a spare room. He was still sound asleep. I left him in darkness and locked the door behind me, while Caleb went to make me some coffee. He brought it to me in the studio, where I felt cold and desolate.

"Please, sir," he said, "there is something I must tell you."

"I am listening," I said.

"Two evenings ago," said Caleb, "Miss van der Horst was seen to go down to the mission at Hlanzeni. She was alone, and she went on foot—as you know, it is generally her custom to ride a horse. Nobody saw her but my sister, who was returning late from a visit. Miss van der Horst did not see my sister. Yesterday morning it was given out that Mr Friston was ill. This morning, at two o'clock, Miss van der Horst was seen climbing out of the window of Zachary's room, by stealth. Everybody knows by now. They are saying that Mr Friston was drugged by Zachary and this woman so that they could blind him to what they were doing. That is all I know. Good-night, sir."

"Good-night, Caleb, and thank you."

I found myself sitting in a chair at Friston's bedside, with only a candle for light. It must have been about half-past nine then. For a long time I sat stock-still. Friston was sound asleep. I don't think I dozed. I must have been in a kind of reverie. After an interminable age I saw that the time by my watch was eleven. The candle was burning much lower. O, and then all at once (it was horrible) I became aware that Friston's eyes were open. They were open. They were fixed on me.

The two eyes of Friston were fixed upon me. He made no more movement than a corpse. If it had not been for the intensity of that gaze I should have allowed myself to suppose him dead. Perhaps he was dead. Perhaps he was in some kind of trance. I found myself wondering, in an access of disinterestedness, what quality it is that is possessed by the human eye alone which gives it that power of penetration; that power to generate an odd sensation of spiritual ecstasy, presumably outside time, space and sex; that power to produce a suggestion of infinite depth and mystery.

These two eyes were only like two dull metal discs. I may have leant forward in my chair, even, with a scientific zeal to examine them. It came upon me that these two eyes, like dull metal discs, like two dull metal discs, were the eyes of Friston. It was that the eyes of Friston—Friston's eyes—were fixed upon me.

There was a little light in them now, and, although Friston seemed to make no more movement than a corpse, his eyes were living eyes. Those two unblinking eyes must have been staring at me for an hour. I felt within me a small surge of fear.

After a very long time I was aware that they narrowed a little. Yes, they were narrowing down a little, as if to determine something.

The faintest of smiles made itself shown on Friston's face. O my God, he was going to say something. He was going to speak a few words of sense. After he had spoken, I supposed (perhaps I was overwrought) he was going to be very ill. I should have to send for a trained nurse from Aucampstroom. But then the only trained nurse in Aucampstroom was Cossie van Honk. She was so soft and obscene, with her cachous and three-inch heels, with her wrinkled face and bitter brittle laughter—I could not do with a harpy in my house. . . .

Now Friston was opening his mouth.

"It's all over, Wolfe," he was saying, "it's all right now."

He closed his eyes. Tight shut, like the eyes of a human being. I sighed with relief. He could recognize me. Perhaps he was sane again.

After a moment he sat bolt upright in bed.

"Give me a dressing-gown. I want to get up and walk about for a time. And I'm ravenously hungry."

I went out and ordered food. Caleb brought in cold meat, bread and butter, and hot coffee.

Friston made an enormous meal, and when he had drunk half his coffee he poured into the cup a quantity of brandy (from a flask I had brought in case of necessity) and finished what was left in the cup at a gulp. Finally he lit himself a cigarette, and then turned to me, after so many vicissitudes, with the same natural air of frankness that I had first noticed in him at Silver Hill.

"I've no reason to be anything but quite open with you," he said, "and I shall tell you plainly what has happened, from the beginning, because I am afraid that you have been put to a lot of trouble on my account. I know what you think. You think I was drugged by Zachary or Mabel, or both, so that I might be put out of the way. You're wrong.

"You saw long ago, I know, my feelings about Mabel. After that last meeting of Young Africa I had the chance of an afternoon alone with her. I wanted to prove to my own satisfaction that she really loved Zachary, and was not just pretending to love him, to taunt me, or for some other unknown feminine reason. We went to the river, and made our way to a thicket in the forest, where there were no sounds but the wind in the trees, the lapping of water and the calling of birds. It was a windy day. We didn't feel the wind where we sat, but we could hear it in the churning tree-tops. Occasionally a leaf or two would fall, turning and turning with a rustling gentleness, taking a long time to fall from the immense height into the primeval stillness below.

'What are we doing here? What the devil is all the mystery about, you bleeding parson?' Mabel asked abruptly with her usual grace. 'You aren't going to lead a poor girl astray?'

"She laughed that rich laugh of hers, and strutted in the glade with columban ease. I can't understand what it is about that woman that prevents her from seeming vulgar. I suppose it is her physical beauty. I have never been jarred in the least by her extraordinary way of talking. It seems part of her.

"Before I could answer her I felt the emotional strain getting the better of me.

'You might have the manners to blush, my bashful curate,' she jeered.

'I don't know what to say to you. You paralyse me,' I said.

'I'll say it for you, my dear,' she said, screwing up her eyes. 'I know what you feel about me. I like you, you fool, but this

Desdemona has found her Othello, so don't expect me to love you.'

"That was all that I went out to hear. I had it from her own lips. She showed some delicacy, I thought, more than I should have expected, in her management of the facts. I felt relaxed, almost joyous, now that I knew where I stood.

"She laughed lightly, and kissed me, warm-breath'd, with real affection, but with the air of fondly indulging a child. We came out of the forest, and away she went on her horse.

"In the evening I found myself at supper, alone with Zachary, by lamplight. The wind had quite gone down and the moon lit the garden with the mild intangible light of a dream. I went early to my room, and sat in a kind of stupor in the reflected moonlight, waiting earnestly for I knew not what.

"After a time I could feel the approach of a crisis—"

(I thought when he said this—said Turbott Wolfe—of my own feelings about Nhliziyombi.)

"—I could feel the approach of a crisis. The moon was veiled. Suddenly I heard, I know not where, the voice of the woman. It was quite soft, and not very near. 'Zachary,' she said. And then I thought I heard, even more distant, inarticulate, the voice of Zachary.

"It must have been a signal that my nerves were waiting for. I leapt up; drew down the blind; struck a match; lit the lamp. The room was illuminated. Under my bed I keep a box. I went down eagerly on my knees and dragged it out. I unlocked it. I took out a pipe specially made for smoking s——. I put it on the table.

"All at once I began shaking like a leaf. It must have been near midnight. The s—— was mixed, I knew, with the virulent flowers of that herb they call m——."

I asked Friston where he got these things.

"O, I just had them: to tell you the truth, I went out secretly and bought them soon after I came to Hlanzeni. I had had a feeling that the time might come when I should need them.

"Now let me tell you what happened. I lit the drug. I did not inhale for a minute, bewildered by the curious unearthly smell. Then I took a first deep draught of the bitter-sweet smoke into my lungs.

"I was torn all at once with a spasm of coughing, but I continued inhaling violently. The coughing had hurt me at first, but after a while it seemed as though I was not coughing myself, but listening to somebody else. I could not feel any pain with the paroxysms. Then I became conscious of a sudden flow of spittle: I was dribbling like a baby. I was watching the lazy smoke in the quiet lamp-lit room. I was slipping away ...

"Music. O, quite unmistakably music. Music played, or uttered, or set in being, terribly fast. Wild, too wild; too maddening. It must be a steam-organ. O yes, it is a steam-organ. There is a merry-go-round. I can only catch glimpses of it through steam and smoke, driven incredibly fast on an unbelievable wind (of which I feel no whisper even) before the merry-go-round, before my eyes. Now and again the flying eddies clear, showing the gold and silver and cherry-rose and ice-green decorations of the whirling merry-go-round: or are they the decorations of the music, or is the music flying along the wind——?

"Yes, and this is Mabel van der Horst. She has grown massive and splendid wings like a swan's. She spreads them out, snow-white, and they quiver. They are like the wings of a bird, and like the wings of a bird she claps them against her flanks.

"Yes, and in a hill-garden unknown to me this must be Zachary who is talking to me in a calm confidential manner, almost severe. He indicates a panorama.

'That,' he says, 'is Aucampstroom.'

The whole country is spread out under my eyes. White roads; varying hills; and rows of poplars like those they had in Flanders before the devastation. And a bleak distant town. There is a charabanc going away quite fast, crowded with people, in a cloud of dust. *Most* realistic.

'Is there anybody I know,' I ask, 'in that car?'

'O yes: Mabel van der Horst.'

She is going away so fast. Where is she going? To Aucampstroom.

"O, the most kaleidoscopic dreams. Portraits of my ancestors; intense perfumes; paddle-steamers; bird's-eye views; bodies and faces; hands; bodies; birds and animals; children; light; colour; curious sensations; embarkation on a paddle-steamer; *vibrements divins de mers virides*; motor-cars; portraits of my ancestors; Gray's *Elegy* . . .

"O, no inconsistencies, I assure you. They are all one. But why should I tell you all this?" Friston asked suddenly. He didn't wait for an answer.

"After a time," he continued, "I find myself actually sitting at luncheon with Zachary and the woman. I am taciturn. This isn't a dream. There is no doubt about this. I return again to my pipe of s——.

"Now it is evening. Zachary appears to be arguing with me in my own room. I don't know why, I'm sure. If he had only known what a fool he was making of himself. And it takes two to make a quarrel, mark you. I must have hit him. We fought. He must have gone out and shut the door.

"And then there were dreams again. Young Africa. Eurafrica. Miscegenation. What uncomfortable ideas for a missionary. And I am a missionary. Perhaps I shall be a patriarch. The father of a half-caste nation, the father of Young Africa; of Eurafrica.

"It is very inconvenient when you don't know who you are, or whether you are one person or two. I was not at all sure of myself once or twice. O no, all the time. But when I opened my eyes and could convince myself that it was really you, Turbott Wolfe (the natives, I said to myself, call him Chastity Wolfe), sitting there in a chair, the very man himself, looking at me quite calmly—when I saw you, I say, and knew you, I knew it was all over, and I felt utterly calm, myself again. I feel quite placid now. Like a lily; like a lamb; like untroubled water. As quiet as a mouse. Calm. Happy.

My room—said Turbott Wolfe—had high whitewashed walls. It seemed as still as the grave when Friston had finished talking. There was not a sound. Friston was contemplating his image in a looking-glass, by candle-light. On Friston's face there was an enigmatic smile.

"I am amused to notice," he said, "that my hair has taken on a tinge of grey since last I saw it in a mirror. But now you must go to bed, Wolfe. I cannot thank you enough for your kindness. To-morrow I return to Hlanzeni. I shall be quite at ease in my heart."

When I left my room early on the following morning I paused to listen to Friston's voice.

> *"They run in the night*
> *With weapons of wood——"*

he was singing within, softly. I opened the door and asked:
"Who?"

He turned on me a mild unstartled gaze.

"The Young Africans, of course," he said in an abstracted voice, "or the Eurafricans.

> *"Dukela, your tide*
> *Is running beveined with the red*
> *Issue of pride——"*

"My good Friston," I said, alarmed, "I don't know in the least what you mean."

"O," he answered, "it is not only the river. It is not only the river Dukela—

> *"The harbour-water runs with blood——*

"It is not only that—

> *"They were decking the bride,*
> *But her lover is dead.*
> *Now her eyes have no sight.*
> *She is standing in terror,*
> *In beauty arrayed——"*

"My dear Friston," I said, in terror myself, "that is really very bad verse."

"It may be," he answered earnestly, "but the meaning is intense. I tell you, the meaning is intense."

After breakfast, Friston walked back to his mission. I wondered if he was mad. It was in the suspicion that he was likely to be permanently deranged that I made up my mind to define as soon as possible the precise attitude of Mabel van der Horst. Before I set out for Mrs Dunford's, Caleb observed to me:

"They are saying at Hlanzeni that Mr Friston is sick in his brain."

"He has been," I said.

Natives are a little too quick to notice and comment on anything amiss. Perhaps it is because they live such open lives themselves. They are strangers to privacy. They do not repress their feelings. They say and do what comes into their heads. They do not turn in upon themselves like the unfortunate Friston. They do not torture themselves to death.

★ 6 ★

At Mrs Dunford's I found Mrs Dunford, in her usual panic and importance.

"O, Mr Wolfe, this *is* a surprise. And what are *you* doing here? *I've* just been to Charlottestown to take Thelma to school. Domestic science. And I came up in the train with a nice minister, Mr Glover. Do you know him? I think he's a nice minister. He was treated very badly by old Frank. He used to try and help old Frank along the road to Jesus. Perhaps it is best that old Frank should have moved along. He was a very sacrilegious old man. Very sacrilegious, he was. O yes, he was that."

I asked if Miss van der Horst was at home?

"O, yes, she's helping me with the house now that Thelma's away so much. I should be very lonely now that the late Mr Dunford has gone before. O well, I daresay Max is happier where he is now. O yes, I should be very lonely if there was no one here to keep me company. Very lonely, I should be. O yes, I should be that. Mabel! Are you there? Let's have some tea. Here's Mr Wolfe."

The door opened, and in came Mabel with a tea-tray.

"I saw you coming, Wolfe," she said, "and got it ready."

There was a plant of cyclamen standing on a table in the window. It was full of flowers. They were of a colour between blood and milk. They must be Mabel's.

"Do you like my flowers?" she asked. "Cyclamen has a sensual beauty, I think."

"I think so, too," said Mrs Dunford. "You're right, Mabel. Cyclamen *has* essential beauty."

It was a puzzle to me how these two women could live peaceably together bottled up in a lonely house. They didn't seem to have anything in common. They were opposites. I asked Mabel for an explanation when we wandered out into the garden together after tea.

"I have to get my living, old boy."

"I should call that evasive, Mabel," I said.

There was an expanse of water in the bottom of the valley below the garden. The surface was glaring and burnished in the sun: it was all scrawled and spattered with the flying, tearing, curving, splashing wings of all kinds of water-fowl. A screaming throng of water-birds, great and small, was floating and hovering all over the fiery lake; and in the wings of those moving, and in their plumage, there was a flicker and sheen of elusive glinting metallic lights, blackish and bluish, full of mystery and foreboding. The birds belonged to another world.

"What on earth brought you up here?" Mabel was asking.

"Well," I said, "if you want to know—I came to tell you that you're driving Friston straight out of his mind. I am going to take the liberty of asking what you're playing at with that nigger?"

"Zachary? I'm going to marry him. And little Friston will get over it. Don't disturb your liver."

"Do you honestly mean to tell me that it's your intention to marry a black man—that nigger?"

"Don't blackguard my Othello, Iago. Have you ever heard of an organization called Young Africa?"

"We're only feeling about for principles, after all," I protested. "If you go and marry a nigger you'll probably break the whole thing up. We might as well have never started Young Africa."

"And what about miscegenation, Mr Turncoat, I'd like to know?" asked Mabel. "I thought that was to be the main idea."

"But Friston's going mad, if he isn't mad already," I said. "It's for his sake that I came up here."

"O, you're an old alarmist," she laughed, "and a turncoat. Friston will get over it. I'm going to talk him round, and ask him to marry Zachary and me himself at the mission. And soon, Wolfe."

She leant forward, laughing, and snapping her fingers.

"Good God," I said.

I played my last card awkwardly.

"Well," I said, "you've driven him to s——, if that's any consolation to you."

"I don't want consoling, you wolf-at-the-door. And s—— is nothing. I used to smoke stacks of it when I was only just out of long clothes."

"There's to be another meeting of Young Africa," I said. "If you come, I hope you'll play the game to Friston. He'll probably be right out of his mind by then."

"Friston's mind seems to be an obsession with you."

"No," I said, "it's his heart."

I went away feeling that I had behaved weakly, and that Mabel knew what she was talking about.

* 7 *

The meeting of Young Africa was held at Silver Hill. Caleb and I were the first to arrive. Mabel came next. I stood nervously at the window, wondering why Friston and Zachary were late, wondering what could have happened to delay them, when they both came round a turn in the garden path, *arm-in-arm*.

Friston looked calm and happy.

"Members of Young Africa," he announced, standing at the head of the table, "this is the third time that our organization has been able to meet. To-day I have a very wonderful and important piece of news to give you. It is news that concerns us all intimately. I will not keep you in suspense any longer. I have the honour to announce the engagement of two of our members—Miss Mabel van der Horst and Mr Zachary Msomi. It is their intention to be married as soon as possible at the church of the Hlanzeni Mission Station, and I count myself particularly fortunate in having been asked by them to perform the marriage ceremony."

The incredible Friston was continuing:

"We may consider the event quite the most significant fruit that has yet been borne by the teachings of Young Africa."

He is very positive, I thought.

"We have always insisted that miscegenation is a misapplied term. Here is a chance for these two members of ours

184

to prove that it is possible for two individuals of different races, one white and the other black, to come together happily and successfully in the most intimate of relationships. Let us unite in wishing them every possible good fortune all their days."

Caleb and I said simultaneously:

"Hear, hear."

4

★ I ★

IT was the second wedding-breakfast that I had seen laid out on the long dining-table in the mission-house at Hlanzeni. This time there were swarms of natives, but no constipated Scandinavians. Mabel looked unlike her usual self with a quiet radiant smile. The only whites from the outside world were myself and Mrs Dunford. She had never been at Hlanzeni before, and commented on the garden with enthusiasm. There was an orange-grove visible from the dining-room windows.

"What megnificint orinches!" she exclaimed.

"The late Mr Dunford," she confided, "didn't approve of missions. He said they teach the natives not to work."

—I had a chance of talking to Friston, who had preached obscurely, but with fervour, at the wedding service.—

"Your sermon interested me immensely," I said. "It was a hazy mixture of sophistry, confused thinking and Bolshevism. I don't know what on earth you mean by all that about habit and instinct. After all, what are instincts but concentrated subconscious hereditary habits? It seems to me that instinct is only a higher form of habit, instead of something quite opposite, as you seem to suggest."

"Poor old thing," said Friston. "And you're very rude. I suppose words are inadequate, or perhaps I find them a medium intractable, or perhaps I am a fool. I can see so clearly always my own meaning, but other people seem to find my words so easy to misinterpret."

"And then," I pursued, "what on earth do you mean by 'America already being given over to the Euramericans'? What on earth is a Euramerican?"

"Wolfe, you are too too blunt. You should use your nerves instead of your brains, and then you would be in the very enviable position of being like me. *Je comprends tout.*"

He began to tell me about a strange dream he had had the night before. He was very animated.

"I have been occupied so long with dreams and visions," Friston said wearily, as though dreams and visions were bed and board to him. "But this dream last night was too ridiculous. There was this man you were telling me about some time ago, Tyler-Harries. God knows why I should dream about him, of all people. I never even saw him. In the dream he kept on measuring off tots of neat whisky and pouring them down my throat, although I kept on assuring him that I don't drink. Then he took out a large notebook, and saying to me: 'Now you are very drunk,' he began to make notes, glancing up at me every now and then. When I asked him what he was writing he just said airily:

'O, statistics. Don't be inquisitive, you little clergingman. I'm not a congregation. Don't suppose that you can bully me.'

"Before I could answer, a loud burst of music appeared at his left hand, rather high up in the air, as intense as a chrysanthemum. Then all at once Tyler-Harries, as large as life, seemed to be receding on a glassy sea, in a little boat, which began to rock violently, and sank suddenly, without warning, like an absurd boat on the stage.

'Aha,' I cried revengefully, 'you would like to leave the sinking ship now, you rat, wouldn't you?'

187

'On the contrary,' asserted Tyler-Harries, waist-high in the water. 'But here is some fruit for you to deliver to Mr Wolfe; the one they call Chastity.'

And he threw me a pomegranate.

'This,' I said, 'as a decorative motif, is a trifle hackneyed.'

But by this time all I could see of Tyler-Harries was his hair, fluffed under the sea's surface like a seaweed; so I got no answer."

"Are you sure it was Tyler-Harries?" I asked Friston, pretending to take him seriously.

'Who else should it be?—And then Mabel came along the beach wheeling with difficulty through the sand a perambulator containing a custard-coloured child.

'Who is this?' I asked.

'Young Africa,' she said, 'or is it Eurafrica?'

'But, quite seriously,' I protested, 'that's not his name?'

'Yes,' she said, 'it's his name. I am going to drown him. He doesn't come up to expectations.'

'Why not let me have him as a souvenir?' I begged. 'I already have a pomegranate. And I could train him as a valet.' ' "

"My good Friston," I said, "I shouldn't let the dreams get on your nerves."

"Dreams? Dreams, you say. O no, not on my nerves. Not at all. You see, the fact is that I am obsessed (I admit that I am obsessed) with dreams and visions, mostly of the future Africa. I do not tell you what I think: I tell you what I feel, which is what I dream, which is what I know. I have reached the pitch of understanding with the nerves. I look forward to the great compromise between white and black; between civilization and barbarism; between the past and the future; between brains and bodies; and, as I like to say, between habit and instinct."

"Friston," I said, "I don't know in the least what you mean. I don't fancy myself as an amateur of philosophy."

"Do you know what Froude said?" Friston asked. "He said that the morality of habit, though the most important element in human conduct, is still but a part of it."

"Friston, I don't care what Froude said." He didn't seem disturbed. I said:

"You seem to know all about Africa. Now what can you tell me about Asia?"

"Ask Russia: or rather, Moscow."

"Indeed, Sir Oracle," I said, annoyed with Friston's everlasting emphatic vagueness. "So you *are* a Bolshevik now?"

"I don't know. But I suspect that the Bolsheviks have some idea of discipline."

"You're very cocksure about everything," I said.

"I am," he declared, with disarming feminine frankness.

I began to wonder if the wedding hadn't been too much for him: I knew of no change in his feelings for Mabel.

"I'm going away from Hlanzeni for a bit," I heard him saying. "I'm leaving to-morrow. I want to spend a week at the river Dukela."

"Where are you going to stay?" I asked. "What are you going to do?"

"I shall swim in the river. I shall talk to the natives, and make notes. I am going to stay at a kraal I have heard about. I've seen the children from the place. They're very charming."

"What is their name?"

"I'm not quite sure of the family name, but their father's name is Langalibalele, and their mother's is—what is it? O yes. Nhliziyombi. It's a curious name."

"It is," I said, "a very curious name. Are you going alone?"

"No. I'm taking one of the mission boys with me."

"Are you going to cross over at all into Swedish East Africa?"

"I don't know," said Friston.

Why was he going to the river? On the evening of the day he left I wandered into my studio. I stood at the window looking at the young moon, blazing with a cold yellow light, the African moon. Perhaps Friston was mad. He was going to the Dukela, he said, to take notes and to swim. He was going to stay at the kraal of Nhliziyombi with her husband Langalibalele. She had been married some years now. Her children I had seen in the store, but Nhliziyombi I had never seen since a certain remote unforgettable afternoon. She knew, and I knew. If she could hear me now I would call to her to come: 'Nhliziyombi.' But she would not come. Her name was a deep wound. I clutched at the window-sill with my fingers.

★ 2 ★

It rained in the night.

Very early in the morning I was out in the garden, and when the sun came up in the east its level marvellous light shone through the sparkling foliage of Ovuzane, upon the very distant broken mountains of Ovuzanyana; upon the in-terfolded foothills, shadowed with dewy patches of forest, and by the mysteries of light divided into cubes of aqueous pink and luminous blue. The trees were virgins laughing with a clear cool gurgle: how shrill and bright the grass!

In a turn of the path I came upon Mabel.

I did not ask myself why she was there. I asked myself, where was her black husband? She was now Mabel Msomi. What could she be doing in my garden? But there she was, in a gown of cream-white, lightly and curiously patterned with black. With each hand she was holding at the tip a leaf of each of the tall tree-ferns that grew on either side of the path. Her teeth were lightly pressed upon her lower lip, as though by them a flight of laughter were imprisoned. Indeed, as I approached, she did laugh a little (to no purpose, I thought) and came a step towards me, suddenly releasing from her fingers the large feathery leaves, from which, sway-ing, glinted speedily earthwards a multitude of raindrops. Her hair, as usual, was clustered round her ears and plaited thickly on the back of her neck, and as usual it had a dark fruit-like lustre. She was beautifully made: broad in the shoul-ders, without gauntness; shapely in arms and legs; fine in both hands and feet, which were large and long. Her carriage had uprightness without stiffness. She moved firmly and flexibly. She always wore low-heeled shoes and seldom a hat.

At sight of her it was a purely physical sensation that over-whelmed me. I said:

"Hullo, Mabel. What the hell are you doing here?"

It was her own idiom.

"Wolfe, you might have the manners to say good-morn-ing."

"O? Van der Horst, you might perhaps acquire the man-ners to call at some time a little nearer sunset than sunrise. And I can't bear facetiousness before breakfast. You haven't answered my question yet."

"Of course I came about Friston," she said earnestly. "He went off yesterday on a —— goose-chase. He's stark staring mad. He's slick out of his mind. I can't think why you let him go."

"Am I my brother's keeper?" I asked.

"I'm absolutely certain he'll never come back. D'you know why he's gone off like this? *He's still in love with me*——"

"O," I said, "you do yourself too much honour."

"Make no mistake, my boy. You'll never see Friston again alive."

"My good Mabel, it's far too early in the morning for such melodrama. Do let us talk of something a little more exhilarating."

"But do you really suppose that I am not serious?" she asked, looking very grave. "I mean every word I say."

"I think you take things too seriously," I suggested. "He told me he was just going to do a little research. At the same time, he is going to enjoy himself walking, and also swimming in the river. It will be a complete change and rest for him. He's very wise to go, especially if he really felt about you as you suggest."

Mabel snorted.

"Mark my words, Mr bloody Philosopher. You make me sick. We shall soon see who's right."

I knew it was she who was right.

Away she went in a rage. She called back:

"If you were a man you would fetch him back, instead of chewing the damn cud like an old cow in your rotten garden."

"It isn't half as rotten as your manners," I shouted. "And I'm not my brother's keeper."

"Say it again, you fool!"

"Mabel, it must be you that are in love with Friston——"

I thought she was out of earshot, but she spat vigorously on the ground.

I allowed myself to reflect that these Colonial girls of very mixed ancestry—not innocent of German blood—perhaps with a touch of the tar-brush, as they say—that girls who could marry blacks——. Yes, but as she walked away in her springing stride, with fine legs and buttocks, and a royal back, out of the early morning shadows into the early morning sun—left, right: left, right—she was no less than a goddess.

As she emerged across the open sward (dew-drenched and sunlit) her departure acquired a colossal valedictory significance: her shadow travelled rapidly with her over the uneven verdure at her left hand (sinister, I thought) and she became the goddess of the future, going out to suffer.

What was her name? Her name was Eurafrica.

* 3 *

When Friston's return was a week overdue, and no word of him had been received, Zachary and Mabel came up to Ovuzane together on horseback, a remarkable pair.

Mabel cried out impulsively in a strange hard voice:

"Wolfe, I told you so."

"What?" I asked, feigning ignorance.

"Friston—you fool."

"Not back yet?" I asked.

"I know he's dead."

"Why, what have you heard?"

193

"Heard? I haven't heard anything. I know."

"O, I say," I mocked. "Second sight?"

"Mr Wolfe," said Zachary, "I have sent people out three times during the last week for news, and all we can hear is that Mr Friston has crossed the border into Swedish East Africa, travelling farther and farther ahead. They say that he seemed in a hurry. I myself want to leave to-morrow in search of him, and I come to ask you to accompany me. I have everything ready at Hlanzeni, and if you will come down there to-morrow afternoon we can make a start."

I went down to Hlanzeni on the following afternoon. Zachary was waiting for me in the dining-room. A meal was laid on the table.

"We shall want some food before we leave," he explained. He held out a packet of letters.

"Now these," he said, "are some letters that have come for Mr Friston. I thought perhaps it would be best for you to open them, in case they tell us any news of him."

"I don't generally read other people's letters," I protested.

"Wolfe," said Mabel, coming into the room, "if you won't open these letters, I shall."

"Good Lord," I exclaimed, "supposing Friston comes back and finds that we've been reading his letters——"

"Well, one of these letters is from the Department of Aboriginal Protection at Aucampstroom. That may easily tell us something. One is from England, and one from Norway. They only came last night. And here is one postmarked Quzo Quza. Isn't that in Swedish East Africa, Zachary?"

"I don't know," he said.

"Anyway," I said, "let us open the letter from Quzo Quza, and leave the others."

"Be damned to you, you obstinate mule," said Mabel,

with her characteristic delicacy. Then she slid her finger under the flap of the envelope from Norway and ripped it open.

I don't know what justification there was for reading these letters. People do strange things when they are excited.

Mabel threw down the letter with an exclamation. I took it up to read. It was as follows:

BERGEN,
10 Sept. 19—.

My dear Mr Friston,

I have heard with the greatest regret of Zachary Msomi's intended marriage to a white woman, Miss van der Horst of Ovuzanyana.

It was kind of you to write and inform me of his intentions, but in your letter I notice a tone of sympathetic enthusiasm which fills me with sorrow. I hope it is not too late to beg of you that you will do your best to discourage the marriage. A long residence of nearly forty years in Africa has convinced me that it is impossible for a white woman to retain permanently the affections of a black man. If the marriage takes place it will certainly be the cause of trouble and suffering.

You must not feel that it is my desire to interfere with the conduct of your work at Hlanzeni. I offer you my advice in the hope that (as it is an old man's) you may find it worth listening to.

You may yourself have already observed that in Africa the contracting parties in such marriages invariably lose entirely the respect of other members of their respective races.—With best wishes,

KARL NORDALSGAARD

The second letter we read was the one from England; again, I confess, read with little justification:

THE PALACE, CROTCHESTER,
12 *Sept.* 19—.

My dearest boy,

You aren't very communicative about Hlanzeni, but I can see from the way you write that you are thoroughly enjoying life. Don't be an ass, like all the missionaries I've ever met. And don't for God's sake end up as a Colonial bishop. They are a repulsive species. So conceited and vulgar.

Your father is getting very pious in his old age. Between ourselves, I don't think he's quite all there. For God's sake don't say I said so.

Harry writes from India that he's having a very good time. I think I told you he's been made A.D.C. to the Governor of Cherribrandi.

Ever your loving

MOTHER

The third letter was the one from Aucampstroom. Its contents were surprising. It was typewritten, in a style that I was unable to admire:

OFFICES OF THE DEPT. FOR ABORIGINAL PROTECTION

AUCAMPSTROOM,
20 *Oct.* 19—.

Rev. Friston,
    Hlanzeni M.S.

Sir,

It has been frequently and forcibly brought to my notice that you have been conducting the Hlanzeni mission in a manner likely to be detrimental to the aboriginal inhabitants of your district, and to the best interests of the Government.

I am not putting it too strongly when I say that I have a very clear case made out against you of what practically amounts to treason, blasphemy, and drunkenness. Even if I was misinformed on these counts, which I am not needless to say, your political propaganda is such unabashed Bolshevism that it alone would suffice to practically remove your status in official eyes.

I suggest that the best chance of trying to rectify your conduct would be best obtained by your interviewing me here personally at your very earliest convenience. If you are unwilling to name a date duty will oblige me to take forcible disciplinary steps immediately with consequences not likely to be too pleasant to yourself.

Awaiting your early reply, I am, etc.,

J. MARSHALL VALDARNO, *Colonel.*

Then there was the letter from Quzo Quza:

QUZO QUZA,
15 *Oct.* 19—.

My dear Friston,

Why didn't you come? It's too late now. Even if you have left before the arrival of this letter it is too late. P. has given the show away, and you can expect to be arrested within a week. I have a vague chance of getting away. If I escape, it will be with the conviction that it will take more than Moscow to organize Africa. M.

We looked at each other.
"It's evidently no use going now," I said.

197

There was a knock at the door.

"It is a telegram," said Mabel, with an intense fear in her eyes. "I suppose he has been arrested."

On the contrary:

ADMINISTRATOR QUZO QUZA *to* HLANZENI MISSION STATION LEMBULAND

personal effects rev rupert friston recovered presumed murdered political or religious reasons by members quzo tribe servant also killed no arrests made yet aucampstroom authorities informed writing.

"Is there an answer?" asked the black sweating telegraph-boy.

We all looked at him with surprise.

"No," I said, "there is no possible answer."

Mabel roughly cleared a space on the garnished table (that had so lately held two wedding-breakfasts) and brought whisky and cigarettes.

There was a knock at the door.

"It is a letter," said Mabel, turning to me, "for you. It's from Colonel Valdarno at Aucampstroom."

It was brought by a mounted policeman. Would I make it convenient to see him on the following day, asked Colonel Valdarno? The man was waiting for an answer. Yes, I wrote, I would make it convenient.

★ 4 ★

There was a barren pear-tree outside the back-door of my home at Ovuzane. When the house-servants had all retired that night, I told Caleb to bring out chairs for us both and set them under the pear-tree. It was now in full leaf, and I lay back to look at it, and at the sky, full of stars.

"Caleb," I said, "I am obliged to give you three months' notice to leave my service."

He did not say a word. Although he was sitting quite close to me I could not even hear him breathe. It was the shock of his life.

"I am going away," I said.

"Why are you going away?"

"Because there is nothing for me to stay for."

"And what is to become of Young Africa?"

"Young Africa, Caleb," I said, "was a device of Miss van der Horst's to justify her marriage to Zachary. But it was also Mr Friston."

"But why, sir, did you have anything to do with Young Africa if it was only what you say? And why did you encourage me——?"

"Who knows, Caleb? Perhaps because of Mr Friston."

"Now he's dead. Couldn't you carry on Young Africa for his sake?"

"No, Caleb."

"I don't understand why, sir."

"My life, Caleb, is like a bucket with no bottom. Nothing can fill it. Once I thought Africa could fill it, but I doubted. Now the lady is married, and has children. Once I thought fame could fill it, but Mr Tyler-Harries, who was going to get it for me, went down to the bottom of the sea—very unreasonably. With Young Africa I allowed myself to be cheated into the idea that politics would give me what I sought. Now, under the barren pear-tree, I see that Young Africa was a monstrous farce. Caleb, I have looked at everything. Perhaps the only thing that satisfies me is my own image in a looking-glass: but even that, perhaps, is not what I want . . . Caleb, I am an egoist."

"And what will you do now, sir?"

"I have just enough money to go and live quietly in England. I shall live in London. I shall dress neatly and inconspicuously, but with distinction. I shall not make many friends. It is not my nature to make many friends. I shall make frequent excursions into the country. I shall design a monument, perhaps, to the unfortunate Mr Friston. I shall dabble in archæology, in church architecture perhaps, or in mediæval domestic economy. I may pay a visit to Russia to study Bolshevism. It will help me to understand a little more about Mr Friston's character. In England I shall be pointed at as an eccentric, because I try and use my brains."

"And what shall I do now, sir?"

"You will marry and settle down in your own country, among your own people, Caleb. You will propagate the species, which any fool can do. I shall make you a present of money before I go, and you will name your first-born after me. You will find happiness and I shall find emptiness, because I have reached a point where life offers nothing but a few sensations, more or less indecent, which I know are only illusions."

* 5 *

The first thing I did on arriving in Aucampstroom the next morning was to arrange with an agent about selling Ovuzane.

"O, we'll have no difficulty in selling it and getting a good price, too," he said. "It is a coveted property, Ovuzane is. I've often had people after it. Occupation in three months from date, you say?"

And at last—said Turbott Wolfe—I found myself outside a door bearing the inscription:

OFFICE OF THE COMMISSIONER FOR
LEMBULAND OF THE DEPARTMENT OF
ABORIGINAL PROTECTION

This is he, I said to myself. This is the day of reckoning.
I am caused to enter.
It was a large bleak room, and very light. The great windows were set in solid chalk-white walls. There was linoleum on the floor; a bench; a cabinet; a safe; an office chair. Behind an immense flat desk whose surface was covered with papers and writing materials sat the Commissioner himself, Colonel Valdarno, like a pimp in a cathedral.

He did not stand up, and bowed without grace. We didn't shake hands.

"Will you take that chair, Mr Wolfe?"
I sat down at the near side of the desk, which lay like a plain between us: and on the horizon, as it were, I contemplated the upper half of Colonel J. Marshall Valdarno.

He was not a tall man, and his head sat awkwardly on his thick red foldy neck, as though it had been thrown there in a hurry by a Creator that had never had time to come back and put it straight. It was a closely-cropped head, with red skin showing through short yellow bristles. The face of the gentleman was clean-shaven, and he lacked eyebrows. His white collar was too tall for fashion and too tight for his red neck, which seemed to have been stuffed into it. His body, in a grey suit, was like a badly-filled bolster. He was an exceedingly uncomfortable-looking man, never at ease.

"I do not think it is necessary," he declared in an awkward magisterial manner, fixing me with his hard gun-metal eyes, and putting the tips of all his fingers together, with his elbows on the arms of his chair; "I do not think it is necessary to tell you, Mr Wolfe, why I have sent for you."

"No?" I said.

"You have heard, I believe, of Mr Friston's death, but before we discuss him there are other things I would like to say. As there are a number of facts—there is a number, I should say—a number of facts to review I must ask you to listen to me, and keep your replies and—er—comments until I have done. I believe I am right in saying that you first took up your residence at Ovuzane in 19—, some years ago now. I was not myself occupying then the position that I now hold, that of Commissioner, but even at that time I was working in this office, under the Department of Aboriginal Protection. I find in my own handwriting the record of a licence having been granted to you in the month following your arrival to trade at Ovuzane, and I think my work—my duty—allows me to say that you can count yourself damn lucky that during all this time your licence has continued unaffected."

"May I remind you," I said, "that I am not in the dock? If you can't be civil I shall have to complain to the Minister."

"O, he won't listen to you now," sneered the Colonel,

tapping some papers on his desk. "Do you know that you've always been, that your—er—activities have always been a source of anxiety to the authorities? Since your first arrival you have always been considered at least unconventional, and public opinion in Lembuland has considered, and still considers you to be eccentric."

"Indeed?" I said. "But I really don't care twopence about 'public opinion in Lembuland'."

"I think this applies not least," Valdarno pursued, frowning, "not least to your ideas about and dealings with the aboriginals that my Department is constituted to protect. As you have been living in a thickly-populated native area it has been thought necessary, during the whole period of your residence at Ovuzane, to have you carefully watched. No doubt you are quite aware of this?"

"No doubt," I said.

"We have to interfere with everybody's private affairs here, as it is a large part of our work—of our duty. But I tell you frankly, Wolfe, that I don't know what you've been playing at."

"I've been earning my living," I said.

"Very likely, Mr Wolfe," Colonel Valdarno laughed efficiently, a hard gun-metal laugh. He was more uneasy than ever. "Very likely. I won't say you haven't; but I daresay you have piled up a nice little fortune at the expense of our unfortunate aboriginals."

"Yes," I said, "I have; though it's none of your business. And I have done it with their goodwill, which is more than your Department ever gets, collecting ridiculous quantities of revenue, for alien purposes, from pauperized blacks."

"Ah, a little rhetoric," sneered the Commissioner, stressing the second syllable of that word. "I'm not going to ask you what you have been up to all these years——"

"I suppose you're going to tell me?" I said.

"What I am going to emphasize is that your more recent political activities have caused my Department a very great deal of anxiety, culminating in the unfortunate end of Mr Friston and this interview here to-day."

"O," I said, "I'm to be made the scapegoat for Friston?"

"For the most part, your political activities, Mr Wolfe, have been as open and clear as daylight, but it is your work in connection with an organization known as Young Africa that has brought you here to-day. I have here a batch of correspondence and other papers which I intend to go through with you. It is my work—my duty. This will be the quickest and most straightforward method of showing you the evidence collected against you. I have letters and statements from your European neighbours, and also evidence provided by our own sources of information."

"By your spies, that is?"

"Mr Wolfe, we have to keep ourselves informed. That's what we're here for. It is our work—our duty. I wish to make it quite clear that no aspersion is cast by my Department upon your personal character: the Minister has seen fit to condemn you simply upon the mass of evidence with which he has been confronted."

Colonel Valdarno fastened upon his red nose, battered out of shape in some native war of the nineteenth century, a steel-rimmed pince-nez. He laughed a gloating automatic laugh, sliding his blunt hands among the papers.

"The very first thing," he announced, screwing up his eyes, "is an original letter from Mr Theodore A. Flesher, a farmer at Ovuzanyana. It is dated not long after your arrival. It runs:

Dear Colonel Valdarno,

I am writing to you personally about a Mr Wolfe, who has for some extraordinary reason been given a licence to trade at Ovuzane. I consider, and I could mention five or six others who also consider, that he is an unfit person to be licensed. I have it as a fact that he spends most of his time in an outhouse, which he has the impudence to refer to as his "studio", with male and female natives in a state of nakedness. What this portends I am unable to say, but if this Mr Wolfe has not already established a house of ill-fame he must certainly indulge in frequent and unbridled licentiousness.

In addition I may add that I have actually seen him with my own eyes in the very act of shaking hands with natives. I have no doubt that illicit liquor trading and other evils are rife: and should be certainly put a stop to.

How such a man came to be licensed I can't imagine, and I could mention five or six others who think the same, and I trust that you will have him closely watched before the White Man's Prestige is trampled any further in the mud.—Yours very truly,

T. A. FLESHER

"A little later," the ugly official continued, shuffling his papers, "in came Mr Bloodfield, another farmer at Ovuzan-yana, into this office in a great state of anger and excitement, with a long story about his sister-in-law. I asked him at the time to give it me briefly in writing, and he did so:

Sir,

Not long since I took Mrs Bloodfield's sister, Miss Smith, to visit Mr Wolfe of Ovuzane Trading Station. He asked Miss Smith to pose as a model for him, as he is an amateur artist, and although I strongly dissuaded her from visiting alone a

man of whom I had not heard good accounts, she insisted on borrow-
ing my car from me, and going over there about a week later by
herself.

She was greatly insulted by this Wolfe, and returned very upset.
I would have gone over to see the man myself, but I knew I should
only be met with further insolence. I was only prevented from going
and giving him a horse-whipping by the knowledge that he was a
newcomer to the district. I should like to have told him what I
thought of him, and I wish to put it on record now that I consider
this Wolfe is an unfit person to be licensed as a trader. He is a dis-
grace to Lembuland.

It is about time your Department kicked this loathsome nigger-
kisser out of our district, if I may say so.—Yours faithfully,

S. S. BLOODFIELD

"Allow this Wolfe to comment," I said, "that Mr Bloodfield's unofficial native wife must have already presented him
at that date with at least two children."

"That's neither here nor there," snapped the Colonel.
"Mr Bloodfield is not a trader."

"My dear Colonel Valdarno," I exclaimed, "you don't
honestly suppose that I should ever look for logic in a government office?"

"There is a collection of letters similar to these two extending over the whole period of your residence at Ovuzane.
The chief point that emerges from them all is a strong disapproval of your relations with, and behaviour towards the
natives. In this respect I don't mind saying that you have always been a thorn in the side of my Department, myself and
the Minister——"

"Which side?" I asked.

"Please hold your tongue, Mr Wolfe."

"Please remember that I am not your prisoner, Colonel Valdarno, nor even your employee."

"And then finally," he said, "there is this disgusting Young Africa business; this loathsome unnatural marriage; and a mad renegade Bolshevik minister. He seems to have dragged you all by the nose in his filthy schemes."

"He wasn't a minister. He was a priest." I said. "I am sick of your opinions. I want to know what the devil you want with me?"

"You do, do you?" he thundered, out of all patience. "I give you three months' notice to quit Ovuzane—lock, stock and barrel!"

"Too late," I said.

"What d'you mean?"

"I mean that I have already made arrangements to leave Ovuzane; to leave Lembuland; to leave Africa. My servants are all under notice: Ovuzane is in the agent's hands."

The Commissioner was plainly disappointed.

"Your departure will be no loss," he said.

"Ask the natives," I suggested, and left the room, and the preposterous buffoon it contained.

Outside I ran into the agent, who was highly excited.

"Ovuzane's sold!" he exclaimed.

"Quick work. Who to?"

"Mr Bloodfield."

★ 6 ★

Let me transfer myself—said Turbott Wolfe—finally and alone to the threshold of the Rev. Justinian Fotheringhay.

For the last time I find myself a step above the street where I stood watching once the deliberate steps of Cossie van Honk, with a hard heart and a soft body retreating in the dusk.

I am standing there for the last time, very deeply moved. Again I put my finger to the bell. It is broken. There is no sound but the humming of a machine two quiet streets away; and the swimming silence subdues a spasm of violent coughing—an old man coughing, choking, somewhere within muffled walls.

I knock at the door. There is a muttered conference within. I am confronted with the large person of Fotheringhay. But, even as I press his hand, his great broad face, his relief-map face, seems far away, very far away; and the small false teeth he shows me for a smile are in a row remote, without the polish of pearls, brittle like white china beads, one as much like another as those things they have on telegraph-poles.

Mrs Fotheringhay stands to receive me in the room on the left. The fingers of one hand are resting lightly on the edge of the table that nearly fills the room, but they are removed to greet me. The coarse cat on the hearth hardly turns its head. It is reviewing its past.

There is the usual fire. The room is stifling. There are the bland scarlet screens.

"Of course you will stay the night? There is no train till to-morrow, and you must give us time to say good-bye. You would be so uncomfortable at the hotel. You shall have The Spare Room. Now Mr Fotheringhay will take you to his study, or on to the verandah, until supper-time. We have an early supper. After supper I shall show you the garden. Do you like gardens? I think they are beautiful."

Mrs Fotheringhay's husband leads me through the french-windows at the end of the room. Until now they had seemed to me like french-windows at the back of a stage, hardly to be used, hardly able to be used, with a gleam not of glass but of talc. Now I see that it is glass.

When we came in again through the french-windows to supper the opposite window gave a view lit by the very late afternoon sun—Aucampstroom gilded. The Dutch church-tower for once is warm and mellow. Shadows, where they are not blue, have an elusive intensity of lilac. Some kind of refraction. It will only last a few minutes.

Supper is calm. The table is broad. I have my back, as usual, to the fire, and the room is very warm: so is the brown soup in wide flattish plates. The spoons and forks are heavy. We are attended by the lean brown Alice in a wide straw hat. *Dira Celaeno*—queen of the harpies.

But the food is good. We have apples for dessert, and then large cups of coffee.

A Cape-cart goes past the house, leaving in the air a trail of gold-dust.

"Now we will go into the garden," Mrs Fotheringhay announces.

She is in her black dress.

She takes my arm.

The most conspicuous thing in the 'garden' is an earth-closet. I have been in there. It is spidery and ramshackle, with a strong smell of sheep-wash.

Here are some seedy cabbages, and a pallid wasted rose.

It is a fine summer evening, but there are only a few moments of twilight.

Here are some dusty macrocarpa trees,

"We planted them fifteen years ago," Mrs Fotheringhay is saying. "There are fourteen, but we call them The Twelve Apostles. This crooked one is Judas Iscariot."

I am in bed. She is playing fanciful old airs on a tinkly old piano to send me to sleep, as if I was a child.

"I shall come and see if you are asleep," she said, twinkling.

Mr Fotheringhay says, the next day:

"I am afraid that piano was wretchedly out of tune last night."

"But Mr Wolfe says it has a beautiful tone," declares his wife.

I have said good-bye to her. The old man accompanies me to the station at dead of night. The station is a little way from the town. We were crossing a waste land. The smallest wind was seething a little in the husky bone-coloured dust-parched grasses: it was seething a little in the moon-bleached waste, at our feet. The path was thick soft dust.

Away to the right there were lighted windows, two or three, masked with black fir-trees, and hardly justified by a muffled hideous laughter at a piano, which is, I guess, being played by Cossie van Honk.

I recognize the midwife's touch. She is assisting the piano to deliver itself of:

"You called me Baby Doll a year ago . . ."

There is a girl at the gate of the same house that contains the piano. She is dressed in white. She is Dutch. She is saying good-bye at great length to a man in the shadows.

All at once there rears itself out of the ground a tall fantastic bridge. It is part of the station. We cross over. We are in the station. We await the train.

The moon has risen. The goods-shed is snow-white on the other side of the line.

I am in the train.

I am lying in bed in a solitary compartment. It is dark. But

I have kept the blinds up, and I can see the moonlight on the deserted barren mountains. They are turning and turning like roundabouts as the train turns round and about. They are turning on turn-tables. The moon and a few stars are flying and turning. I am falling asleep. I have found a quotation:

> "*Into the night, into the blanket of night,*
> *Into the night rain gods, the night luck gods,*
> *Overland goes the overland passenger train.*"

APPENDIX I

AMONG Friston's papers—said Turbott Wolfe to me before he died—I found some notes for a diagram he was going to prepare. The figure was described as follows:

THE POLITICO-ÆSTHETE

a man, fortunate or unfortunate, whose existence is hemmed in by wireless telegraphy ('then', as the newspapers say, 'in its infancy'). He staggers, poor man, under the weight of the past; and he struggles, poor man, under the load of the future. He has not got over the French Revolution when he is faced with the Russian. He has not digested the Renaissance before he is confronted with Cubism. Dadaism he finds easier. He would like to focus his attention on the point where the rational in his character coincides with the concupiscible; but is it really his character, he wonders——?

He is divided by a thin red line drawn down the middle. On the right hand he is politico, on the left æsthete. His left eyelid droops in languor, heavy and sallow over the brightest of eyes; his right eye is fastened irrevocably upon the main chance. While his right foot is firmly seated on a money-bag (marked in green ink "8% interest charged on overdue accounts"), his left balances him not too easily on a bag of other people's dirty washing.

How attentive his right ear seems to the vivid cacophony of the Austrian National Anthem proceeding from a hurdy-gurdy at the corner of Park Lane and the long, long trail. But his left ear is devoted to a saxophone (or is it a sexophone?)

upon which is subtly rendered by a young man from Cardiff with a Polish name a tune called:

"*A-be, A-be, my boy, what are you waiting for now?*"

Under his left arm are the complete works of Freud, and under his right the *Almanach de Gotha* ('now defunct', as the newspapers say). The Newspapers? O yes, in his right hand please find enclosed *John o' London's Weekly*; and in his left a 'slim volume', very privately printed: yes, and in his left there is also (much less slim) a book of luggage-tags (what you and I call labels) quite ready to be tied to anything, innocent or guilty. Let us pray that the Politico-Æsthete will be merciful with his labels.

In his buttonhole there is no carnation, no sunflower—but a unique dahlia.

His right-hand pocket is full of slogans; and his left-hand of epigrams. The slogans are not worth printing, and the epigrams are unprintable . . .

"Post-War," murmurs the Politico-Æsthete . . .

APPENDIX II

AMONG Friston's papers there were also three poems. They may not have much value as poetry, but they are interesting psychologically: one can, I think, assign them their places in Turbott Wolfe's story.

THERE IS NO COMING BACK

A gesture, and she went
Away without a word.
    Summer leaves, unstirred,
The only monument
    Of sounds unheard.

O, time and space went down,
And worlds were won, and more
    Worlds were lost before
The flutter of her gown,
    The flower she wore.

There is no coming back,
For she, in going, knew
    How fervent and how few
Sounds then could silence lack:
    Nor spoke anew.

TURBOTT WOLFE

[1] A STRANGER AT THE WEDDING[1]

Shall soul and sense unite
Now, at the beginning?
Or those two find delight
Bloom slowly, winning
Their spiritual home
Like honey from the comb?

That is for them to know,
But (bell with bell ringing)
I must gladly bestow
(O hear the singing!)
A kiss of peace, in prayer,
Upon the bridal pair.

MANIFESTO

BY A MAN IN A TRAP

With monkey-shadows on a screen
You mock me now, but I can wait.
I cease to be, as I have been,
Intimidated by a fate.

[1] Reprinted, by permission, from the Zulu national newspaper, *Ilanga lase Natal*, where it first appeared.

W. P.

TURBOTT WOLFE

I yawn, when I was used to wince,
At such clandestine vileness done—
Fear has withered swiftly since
HORROR was written on the sun.

Doors, mouths, and periods open, shut:
Time will not give what time has lacked.
I am constrained to play a part—
An actor, only free to act.

THE END

MORE TWENTIETH-CENTURY CLASSICS

Dead Man Leading

V. S. Pritchett

Introduction by Paul Theroux

An expedition to rescue a man missing in the Brazilian jungle becomes a journey of self-discovery for his son. Conradian in conception, the treatment in the novel of obsession, verging on madness, is strikingly original.

'a rich, original and satisfying book'—*Spectator*

The Secret Battle

A. P. Herbert

Introduction by John Terraine

First published in 1919, *The Secret Battle* is an account of the wartime experiences of an infantry officer, Harry Penrose, as he is tested and brought to breaking-point, first in Gallipoli, then with his young wife in London, and finally in the trenches of France. Without melodrama or sensationalism, Herbert conveys the full horror of war and its awful impact on the mind and body of an ordinary soldier.

'This book should be read in each generation, so that men and women may rest under no illusion about what war means.'—Winston Churchill

Elizabeth and Essex

Lytton Strachey

Introduction by Michael Holroyd

Lytton Strachey achieved fame with the publication in 1918 of *Eminent Victorians*; but none of his books brought him greater popular success than his last: this dramatic reconstruction of the complex and stormy relationship between Queen Elizabeth I and the dashing, if wayward, Earl of Essex.

'a brilliant and insufficiently appreciated book'—A. L. Rowse

The Fifth Queen

Ford Madox Ford

Introduction by A. S. Byatt

Ford Madox Ford's vision of the court of Henry VIII brilliantly recreates the struggle between Henry's fifth wife, Katharine Howard, and the tough, unscrupulous Thomas Cromwell for the mind and soul of their King.

'The best historical romance of this century.'—*Times Literary Supplement*
'magnificent'—Graham Greene

His Monkey Wife

John Collier

Introduction by Paul Theroux

The work of this British poet and novelist who lived for many years in Hollywood has always attracted a devoted following. This, his first novel, concerns a chimpanzee called Emily who falls in love with her owner—an English schoolmaster—and embarks on a process of self-education which includes the reading of Darwin's *Origin of Species*.

'John Collier welds the strongest force with the strangest subtlety . . . It is a tremendous and terrifying satire, only made possible by the suavity of its wit.'—Osbert Sitwell

'Read as either a parody of thirties' fiction or just crazy comedy, it deserves its place as a 20th-century classic.'—David Holloway, *Sunday Telegraph*

The Village in the Jungle

Leonard Woolf

Introduction by E. F. C. Ludowyck

As a young man Leonard Woolf spent seven years in the Ceylon civil service. The people he met in the Sinhalese jungle villages so fascinated and obsessed him that some years later he wrote a novel about them. It is his knowledge and profound understanding of the Sinhalese people that has made *The Village in the Jungle* a classic for all time.

'The Village in the Jungle is a novel of superbly dispassionate observation, a great novel.'—Quentin Bell

They were Defeated

Rose Macaulay

Introduction by Susan Howatch

In her only historical novel, the author of *The Towers of Trebizond* skilfully interweaves the lives of Robert Herrick and other seventeenth-century writers with those of a small group of fictional characters.

'To the great enrichment of the English language Miss Macaulay has chosen an historical subject. As a result she has achieved her greatest success—which means she has added something permanent to English letters.'—*Observer*

'One of the few authors of whom it may be said she adorns our century'—Elizabeth Bowen

Seven Days in New Crete

Robert Graves

Introduction by Martin Seymour-Smith

A funny, disconcerting, and uncannily prophetic novel about Edward Venn-Thomas, a cynical poet, who finds himself transported to a civilisation in the far future. He discovers that his own world ended long ago, and that the inhabitants of the new civilisation have developed a neo-archaic social system. Magic rather than science forms the basis of their free and stable society; yet, despite its near perfection, Edward finds New Cretan life insipid. He realizes that what is missing is a necessary element of evil, which he feels is his duty to restore.

'Robert Graves' cynical stab at creating a Utopia is a poetic *Brave New World* filled with much more colour and dreaming than the original *Brave New World* of Aldous Huxley.'—Maeve Binchy

The Aerodrome

Rex Warner

Introduction by Anthony Burgess

Published nearly a decade before Orwell's *1984* shocked post-war readers, *The Aerodrome* is a book whose disturbingly prophetic qualities give it equal claim to be regarded as a modern classic. At the centre of the book stand the opposing forces of fascism and democracy, represented on the one hand by the Aerodrome, a ruthlessly efficient totalitarian state, and on the other by the Village, with its sensual muddle and stupidity. A comedy on a serious theme, this novel conveys probably better than any other of its time the glamorous appeal of fascism.

'It is high time that this thrilling story should be widely enjoyed again'—Angus Wilson

'It is a remarkable book; prophetic and powerful. Many books entertain but very few mange to entertain and to challenge at such a deep level.' *Illustrated London News*

The Unbearable Bassington

Saki

Introduction by Joan Aiken
Illustrated by Osbert Lancaster

Set in Edwardian London, Saki's best-known novel has as its hero the 'beautiful, wayward' Comus Bassington, in whom the author invested his own ambiguous feelings for youth and his fierce indignation at the ravages of time.

'There is no greater compliment to be paid to the right kind of friend than to hand him Saki, without comment.'—Christopher Morley